165 miles ... ennine Way
from He... drian's Wall

Heart of the Pennine Way

Best wishes
Chris & Tony
Grogan

Tony & Chris Grogan

SKYWARE PRESS 2015

Hebden Bridge to Hadrian's Wall

1. **Hebden Bridge to Ickornshaw** (16.8 miles / *27.1 km*) 11
2. **Ickornshaw to Malham** (17.5 miles / *28.1 km*).....................................16
3. **Malham to Horton-in-Ribblesdale** (14.8 miles / *23.8 km*)..................22
4. **Horton-in-Ribblesdale to Hawes** (13.6 miles / *21.9 km*).....................28
5. **Hawes to Tan Hill** (16.3 miles / *26.2 km*)...34
6. **Tan Hill to Middleton-in-Teesdale** (16.6 miles / *26.7 km*) 40
7. **Middleton-in-Teesdale to Dufton** (20.2 miles / *32.5 km*) 48
8. **Dufton to Alston** (19.3 miles / *31.1 km*) 56
9. **Alston to Greenhead** (16.6 miles / *26.7 km*).......................................62
10. **Greenhead to Housesteads & Bardon Mill** (12.9 miles / *20.8 km*) 68

APPENDIX: Unfinished Business 74

Pennine Way South: **Edale to Calder Valley** (42.5 miles / *68.4 km*) 74

Pennine Way North: **Housesteads to Kirk Yetholm** (53.1 miles / *85.4 km*)...78

Introduction - Why the Mid Pennine Way?

For some 50 years hardy hikers have been undertaking the gruelling challenge of the Pennine Way, walking from Edale in Derbyshire to Kirk Yetholm on the Scottish Borders. Each year an estimated 2,000 or so complete the journey; others abandon the challenge at an early stage, the going proving too tough.

For many walkers these days, the prospect of a three-week, 268-mile trek along the high Pennine moors and mountains - *the backbone of England* – is just too daunting. Nowadays there are many other long-distance trails vying for attention, almost all a good deal easier, both physically and logistically. The Pennine Way has somewhat fallen from favour.

In 1996 Chris and I began planning our annual fortnight's walking holiday and turned our attention to the Pennine Way. We knew we couldn't fit it all in, but what to leave out?

To be honest it was a no-brainer. We'd read plenty of frightening accounts of the struggles to cross the boggy wastes of the Derbyshire Black Peak, with walkers sinking thigh deep into the glutinous bogs of Kinder Scout, Bleaklow and Black Hill. We didn't fancy that. Nor were we drawn to the prospect of a 27-mile marathon slog along the boggy ridge of the Cheviots on the final day.

So we settled on an abridged version of the National Trail, a sort of *Pennine Way Lite*. We opted for a 165-mile trek along the very heart of Britain's premier National Trail, which we called the **Mid Pennine Way**.

Later that summer we set off with some trepidation from Hebden Bridge for Haworth. Bronte country proved inspiring.

Next morning the sun was shining and we skipped across the familiar rough moorland pastures forming the northern edge of the South Pennine range, stopping overnight at Earby hostel before descending to cross the Aire Gap at Gargrave, finishing a fairly easy day with a gentle riverside ramble to magnificent Malham. We were now in the Yorkshire Dales.

Next day was our first real test, the two mountains of Fountains Fell and Pen-y-ghent, but all went well and after a break at Horton-in-Ribblesdale we were heading north again along the bright limestone scars of Ribblesdale. We enjoyed a brief reunion with the Dales Way on Cam High Road before dropping into the top of Wensleydale and the busy market town of Hawes.

We made a short diversion to visit Hardraw Force – the country's highest waterfall – before the steady climb over Great Shunner Fell and down into the glorious deep cut valley of Swaledale. The hostel in Keld offered another fond reunion – this time with Wainwright's Coast to Coast path.

We were by now fully immersed in the Pennine Way experience, enjoying the nearest thing to wilderness walking that England has to offer.

Beyond Tan Hill and England's highest pub, we left the Yorkshire Dales to yomp quite cheerfully across the bogs of Sleightholme Moor to Bowes, before another shortish day crossing Baldersdale and Lunedale brought us to Middleton-in-Teesdale.

We were a bit anxious about the next two days – which promised to be both long and tough, but beautiful Teesdale proved to be one of the highlights of the whole expedition: dramatic waterfalls, big empty moorland and the stunning spectacle of High Cup Nick.

An overnight stay at the hostel in lovely little Dufton saw us set off refreshed for the climb to the Pennine's highest peak – Cross Fell. It was shrouded in mist, so there was not much to see, but we survived the steady climb up and enjoyed the long walk down to Garrigill and on to Alston.

We lingered in England's highest market town, watching the tiny steam trains come and go, before finally setting off on the long trek along the South Tynedale valley and across the marshy pastures of Hartleyburn and Blenkinsopp Commons.

Our final day was a sheer delight, hopping along Hadrian's Wall atop the impressive Whin Sill ridge, before spending an afternoon exploring the fascinating Roman forts at Housesteads and Vindolanda. We caught the train at Bardon Mill for Carlisle and then onto the Settle-Carlisle line home.

Hadrian's Wall 1996. Standing on the wall these days is a definite no-no

We had thoroughly enjoyed our Mid Pennine Way adventure and for Chris that was enough. But I couldn't shake of a niggling feeling of *unfinished business* and so felt compelled eventually to revisit the Pennine Way and tick off those two end stages.

They were tough going for sure, but perhaps not surprisingly they proved much less scary than I had imagined. The notorious bogs have long since been tamed with mile upon mile of stone slab paving. I managed to break the 27-mile trek over the Cheviots mid-way, dropping from the ridge to be picked up courtesy of the good folk who run the excellent Forest View Walkers Inn at Byrness.

So, if you are one of those many walkers who have considered walking the Pennine Way, but have been put off because it is too long and too tough, then please think again. It needn't be an all-or-nothing gruelling expedition. Enjoy instead a fortnight's trek along the heart of Britain's premier National Trail.

We would very much like to recommend the **Mid Pennine Way** to you.

Tony & Chris Grogan

Walking the Mid Pennine Way

The Mid Pennine Way covers 165 miles from Hebden Bridge to Hadrian's Wall along the heart of Britain's premier National Trail.

It is formed by taking the two end stages of the Pennine Way, undoubtedly the most difficult stages both physically and logistically, and putting them to one side. That cuts out *Edale to the Calder Valley* and *Hadrian's Wall to Kirk Yetholm*, a total of just under 100 miles. The remaining 165 mile route is a glorious trail along the backbone of England, from the wild moors of West Yorkshire to the rich southern borders of the Northumberland National Park.

It includes almost all the highlights to be found along the Pennine Way, including the stunning limestone country of the Yorkshire Dales, the dramatic waterfalls and wild open moors of the Durham Dales and the very best of the Hadrian's Wall World Heritage Site.

Both the start at the beautiful and lively South Pennine mill town of Hebden Bridge, and the finish at the tiny Northumberland village of Bardon Mill, are easily reached by mainline rail from both west and east. There is plenty of good quality accommodation and facilities along the way to suit most tastes.

The Mid Pennine Way is still a tough walk. Although in distance it's only about 65% of the full National Trail, make no mistake, the challenge is 100% Pennine Way. The key to success is careful preparation.

This book divides the walk into the traditional 10 sections. Strong and experienced fell walkers may tackle one section a day, but for most walkers some sections are just too long. It's better to break them and take time to explore. 12 to 14 days make better itineraries, including a couple of shorter half days, whilst still allowing the walk to fit into a fortnight slot.

The first two sections can be conveniently broken into three, with stopping points at Ponden or Haworth and at Earby or Gargrave. Section 5 can be broken at Thwaite, Muker or Keld, especially if the next goal is Bowes (though check first that accommodation is available there). Section 6 can be conveniently broken at Langdon Beck, especially given the tough day to follow, leaving plenty of time then to enjoy the facilities of Middleton-in-Teesdale and the waterfalls along the way.

If accommodation is available in Garrigill, then Section 7 can be broken here – there are further options to break Section 8 at Slaggyford or Burnstones, and the prospect of the South Tyne Railway being extended from Alston to Slaggyford and beyond in the near future opens more possibilities.

Finally, if time permits, it can be very rewarding to seek accommodation at or around Bardon Mill at the end – possibly at Once or Twice Brewed – thereby giving ample time to fully explore the Roman sites of Housesteads, Vindolanda and surrounding areas.

An increasingly popular way to tackle long distance walks is by breaking them into stages of between 3 to 5 days each, using public transport to access each stage. This increases the chances of being able to pick good weather.

The Mid Pennine Way can be easily divided into 3 stages using the railway, most notably the Settle-Carlisle line – the most scenic in England - to access each stage.

***The Settle to Carlisle line** - the most scenic in all England - runs from Leeds to Carlisle and can be used to access the Mid Pennine Way at key stages.*

Stage 1: Hebden Bridge to Horton-in-Ribblesdale or Hawes (using the bus link to Garsdale station);

Stage 2: Horton-in-Ribblesdale or Hawes to Dufton (using a taxi or walking the extra 3 miles to Appleby-in-Westmorland);

Stage 3: Dufton to Housesteads and Bardon Mill (as above).

The strip maps in this guide are aligned in the general direction of travel, which varies from map to map. The main maps are based on OS Explorer maps at a scale of 1:25,000, but with superfluous detail omitted and with some features exaggerated for clarity. The route has been surveyed on the ground prior to publication, but bear in mind that the countryside changes – new fences appear, stiles are replaced by gates, signs disappear.

The main route is shown together with official alternatives such as the Bowes Loop, as well as some other popular alternatives.

Your experience of the trail will largely be determined by the weather. As the photos in this book show, the sun always shines on Mid Pennine Way walkers – but only the very lucky ones. Most people will get rained on some of the time; some people will get rained on most of the time. So carry a good set of waterproofs and extra layers alongside the sun block. Carry plenty of water and enough food for a full day.

A compass or GPS are absolutely essential for misty conditions which you are almost certain to encounter at some stage on the exposed upland moors and fells, and a mobile phone can be useful in emergencies – although you may not always get a signal. If you get into trouble on the fells, at the first opportunity call 999 and ask for the **Police**, then tell them you need **Mountain Rescue**.

Information about any route changes, accommodation, other resources, etc. can be found on the associated website at:

www.midpennineway.uk

Those wishing to finish the full Pennine Way, will find the end sections in the appendix.

A brief history of the Pennine Way

The Pennine Way was opened in April 1965 as Britain's first official long distance trail.

It was the brainchild of Tom Stephenson – socialist campaigner, pioneer of the ramblers' movement and a key figure in the eventual establishment of the National Parks and our *right to roam*.

In 1935 two American girls wrote to Tom Stephenson, then Rambling correspondent for the Daily Herald, asking if there was anything in England like America's 2000-mile Appalachian Trail. This prompted Stephenson to write an article for the paper entitled *Wanted – A Long Green Trail*, in which he outlined his plan for *a Pennine Way from the Peak to the Cheviots*.

The article generated a lot of public interest and in 1938 the *Pennine Way Association* was formed and began the process of drafting a detailed route*. Most of the proposed 250-mile route followed existing rights of way. Just over 50 miles crossed land where access was denied, and most of this fell in the Peak District.

It was no accident that Stephenson chose to start the Pennine Way at Edale. For years the grouse moors of Kinder Scout and Bleaklow had been vigorously denied to walkers by land owners. In 1932 over 400 people participated in a mass trespass onto Kinder Scout. Five men from Manchester, including the leader, Benny Rothman, were subsequently jailed.

The Second World War intervened, with 1945 bringing an unexpected landslide victory for a radical Labour government under Clement Atlee. The post war reconstruction saw the birth of the National Health Service and the Welfare State, as well as the nationalisation of major industries.

In May 1948, at the instigation of Hugh Dalton MP, Stephenson led a group of key Labour Party politicians on a three day walk along the proposed Pennine Way from Middleton-in-Teesdale to Housesteads on Hadrian's Wall. It was enough to convince Dalton and in July 1951, whilst minister for local government, he officially approved the creation of the Pennine Way, which he hoped would be open within a year.

Planning the Pennine Way route, Birkdale Farm, Upper Teesdale, 1948. From left: Barbara Castle MP, Fred Willey MP, Arthur Blenkinsop MP, George Chetwynd MP, Tom Stephenson, Hugh Dalton MP and Julian Snow. (Photo courtesy Dalesman Magazine)

In fact the trail was to languish through Labour's *thirteen wasted years* until Harold Wilson's premiership in 1964, when the Pennine Way was finalised and officially opened at an event on Malham Moor on April 24 1965, attended by over 2,000 people.

The Youth Hostels Association opened a series of new hostels along the route especially to service Pennine Way walkers (sadly, many have since closed, though a few continue as independent hostels).

Amongst the first guide books to appear were Christopher Wright's *A guide to the Pennine Way* (1967) and Tom Stephenson's own *The Pennine Way* in 1969. The most popular was undoubtedly Alfred Wainwright's quirky *Pennine Way Companion* published in 1968.

Wainwright didn't enjoy the Pennine Way much, being dogged by bad weather most of the time. He struggled particularly with the

** For a detailed account see Chris Sainty's "The Pennine Way - A Walker's Guide" (DB Publshing 2014).*

two end stages; at Black Hill he sank into a bog and had to be rescued with the help of a passing Park Warden. Wainwright noted: *Arrival in the valley of the Calder marks a definite stage of the Pennine Way. Behind now are the lonely peat moors, a desolate and inhospitable region.*

Wainwright also thought the start and finish points should have been different: *Better that the Pennine Way had been given the glorious entry to the hills provided by charming Dovedale as its starting point, and, as its thrilling finale, the exciting arrival at the Roman Wall!*

The Pennine Way proved to be a great success. A Countryside Commission report claimed that by 1990 12,000 long-distance walkers and 250,000 day-walkers were using all or part of the trail per year. The attrition rate, though, was high – it has been suggested that in the early years more than half of those setting out from Edale abandoned the walk at an early stage.

With thousands of walkers' boots taking a toll on the fragile peat bogs, the Pennine Way became a victim of its own success. By 1989 the average eroded width of the route was over 4 metres. A solution was found in the laying of thousands of large stone flags brought from the floors of demolished Lancashire cotton mills – ironically the same mills that produced many of the early pioneering ramblers. In the decade from 1991 to 2001 more than £1.4 million was spent repairing over 16 miles (26 km) of the Pennine Way.

The strategy worked and the rare and fragile environment began to recover. The route also became much easier to navigate for walkers, but for some it meant the loss of a sense of a true *wilderness walk*.

The Pennine Way was the first of 15 National Trails in England and Wales. Its launch also encouraged the creation of a number of popular *unofficial* long distance trails, including the **Dales Way** (1969) devised by Colin Speakman and Tom Wilcock of the West Riding Ramblers, and Wainwright's own **Coast to Coast Walk** (1973).

The Pennine Way and other National Trails are overseen by Natural England, but recently responsibility for managing and maintaining each trail was passed to a partnership of the local authorities along each route. In 2015 the Yorkshire Dales National Park Authority became the lead partner for the Pennine Way.

There have been a few changes to the route over the years, but nothing fundamental. Erosion meant that the main crossings of Kinder Scout and Black Hill had to be diverted onto what were originally alternative *bad weather* routes. The total distance of 268 miles usually given includes the Bowes Loop; the direct distance, including the diversion to the Cheviot, is about 260 miles.

The Pennine Way is rightly regarded as one of the toughest long distance trails in the country, and with plenty of other long distance trails to choose from, this has led to a steady decline in the numbers of walkers tackling the whole route, now something under 2,000 annually. But some sections prove much more popular than others. *People counters* along the route show day walkers and weekend walkers favour the more popular sections at Malham, Teesdale and Hadrian's Wall.

The way people choose to walk long distance trails is also changing: some break the trail into shorter stages; some use the services of professional walk guides, holiday companies and baggage couriers to ease the way.

In 2012 the Pennine Way gained additional notoriety as the route of *Britain's most brutal race*; the **Spine Race** is run in mid winter and competitors have just seven days to cover the 268-mile trail.

2015 marks the 50th anniversary of the Pennine Way, an event celebrated with BBC TV and radio documentaries, a series of *Walk the Way in a Day* walks, the launch of the Hebden Bridge Loop and the publication of this guidebook.

Winter view from Heptonstall across the Calder valley to Stoodley Pike

Canal side

Approaching Top Withir

Packhorse Bridge - starting point

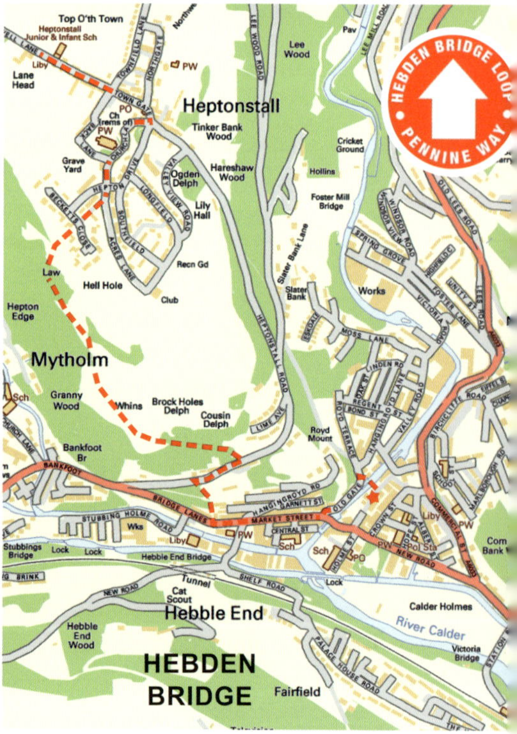

Section 1: **Hebden Bridge to Ickornshaw**

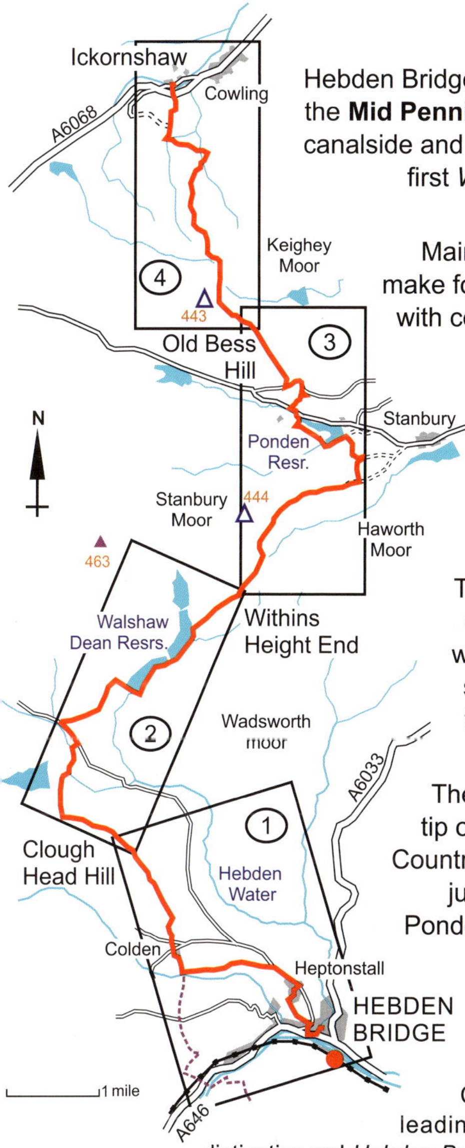

16.8 miles (*27.1 km*)

Hebden Bridge in the Calder Valley makes a great start to the **Mid Pennine Way**. This old mill town with its colourful canalside and thriving alternative culture became Britain's first *Walkers Are Welcome* town in 2007 and has everything a walker needs.

Mainline train links from Leeds and Manchester make for easy access to the town, which is packed with cosy pubs and cafes, restaurants and shops. There's a flourishing arts scene supporting several art galleries, a cinema, theatre and the renowned music venue - the Trades Club. There's a good mix of accommodation with hotels, B&Bs and an independent hostel.

The local Walkers' Action group have helped establish a brand new *Hebden Bridge Loop* which links to the Pennine Way. Launched in spring 2015 to mark the 50th anniversary of the National Trail, this is utilised as the start of the Mid Pennine Way.

The first section takes you across the northern tip of the South Pennine moors, through Bronte Country to Ickornshaw. It's quite a long first day at just under 17 miles, but you can break this at Ponden, with nearby Stanbury offering additional accommodation and a bus link to Haworth.

Start in the pedestrianised **Bridge Gate** by the 16th century packhorse bridge which spans Hebden Water and gives the town its name.

Cross the bridge and turn left along **Old Gate** leading right onto **Market Street**, following the distinctive red *Hebden Bridge Loop* waymarks. Watch for a right turn onto **Stoney Lane** and a steep climb up the Cuckoo Steps to **Heptonstall Road**. Turn right up the road for 100 metres and join a public footpath on the left which leads steeply up northwest on a cobbled track into woods. Soon superb views open out across the Calder Valley.

Steps lead up to the left of the quarry at Hell Hole and into a snicket. Cross the first road, along the snicket, then turn left on **Acres Lane**, across **Becketts Close** heading towards St Thomas's Church. Bear right past the church and squeeze between buildings to come out down **Church Lane** and turn left to climb the cobbled **Towngate** through Heptonstall.

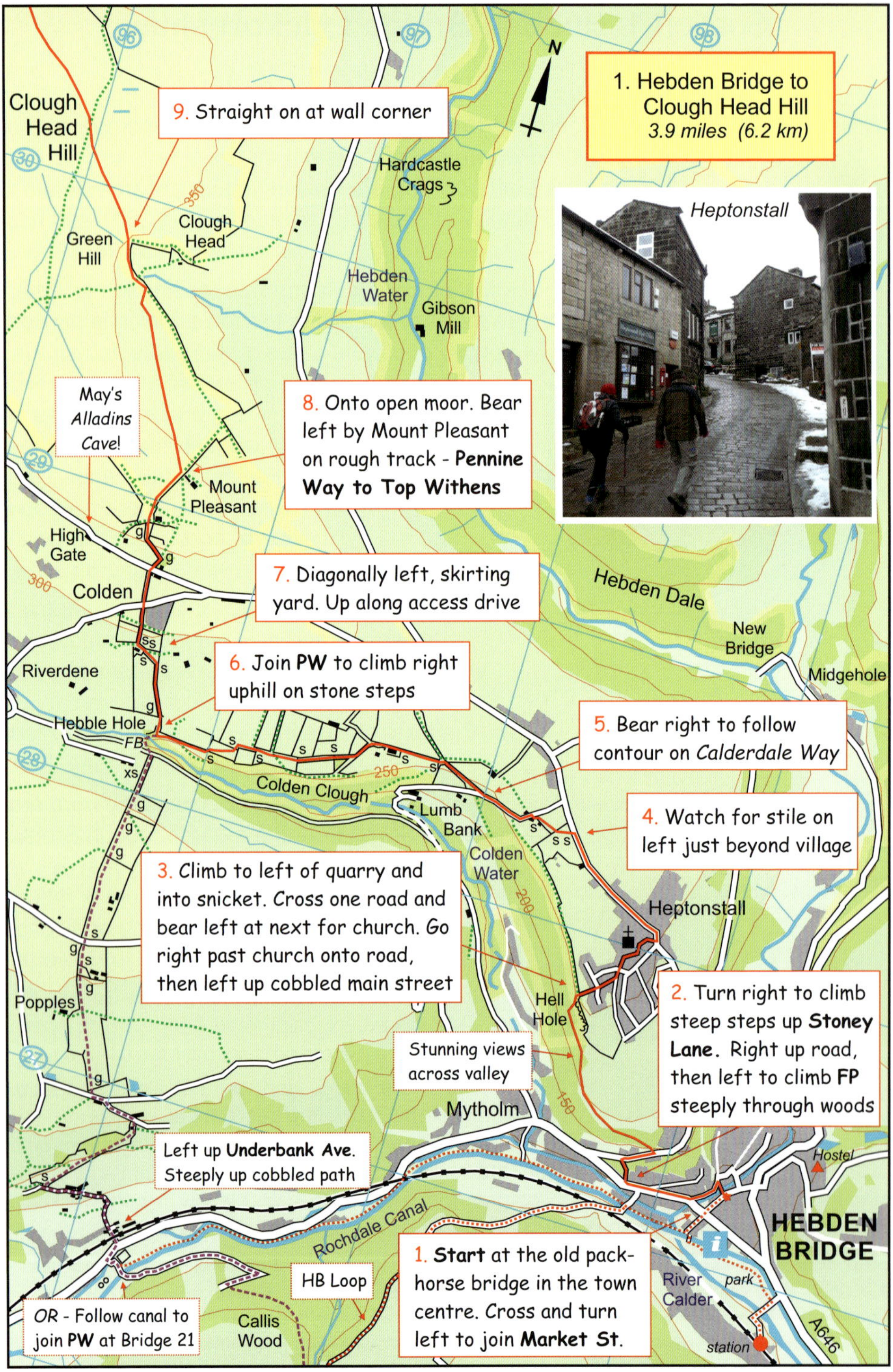
1. Hebden Bridge to Clough Head Hill
3.9 miles (6.2 km)
Heptonstall
1. Start at the old pack-horse bridge in the town centre. Cross and turn left to join Market St.
2. Turn right to climb steep steps up Stoney Lane. Right up road, then left to climb FP steeply through woods
3. Climb to left of quarry and into snicket. Cross one road and bear left at next for church. Go right past church onto road, then left up cobbled main street
4. Watch for stile on left just beyond village
5. Bear right to follow contour on Calderdale Way
6. Join PW to climb right uphill on stone steps
7. Diagonally left, skirting yard. Up along access drive
8. Onto open moor. Bear left by Mount Pleasant on rough track - Pennine Way to Top Withens
9. Straight on at wall corner
May's Alladins Cave!
Stunning views across valley
Left up Underbank Ave. Steeply up cobbled path
OR - Follow canal to join PW at Bridge 21
HB Loop
Clough Head Hill
Green Hill
Clough Head
Hardcastle Crags
Hebden Water
Gibson Mill
Mount Pleasant
High Gate
Colden
Riverdene
Hebble Hole
FB
Colden Clough
Lumb Bank
Colden Water
Hebden Dale
New Bridge
Midgehole
Heptonstall
Hell Hole
Popples
Mytholm
Rochdale Canal
Callis Wood
River Calder
park
station
Hostel
HEBDEN BRIDGE
A646
N

Beyond the village a stile on the left leads across two fields and out onto a walled lane beside a house. Follow the lane down to the left. Go straight on where it forks later downhill to the left.

Care is needed navigating now along the *Calderdale Way* as it follows the contour above the woods heading west. Finally the path drops left into the woods, and as the path begins to descend to the beck at Hebble Hole it meets a set of stone steps on the right, marking the **Pennine Way** proper.

Follow the Pennine Way climbing north across fields and out onto open moor at Clough Head. The path is unclear at first as it heads northwest, but soon stone flagging shows the way.

The path drops to pass Gorple Reservoir and down to Clough Foot, which is a popular spot for a break. The path climbs above the east bank of Graining Water which it follows north before turning right to join the road northwest along the Ridge.

At a fork the route cuts back right to follow the Calder-Aire Link Road to the Walshaw Dean Reservoirs. The path now follows the south eastern banks of the lower and middle reservoirs, before cutting off right along a track at a stone bridge, then right again along a slabbed path for Top Withins.

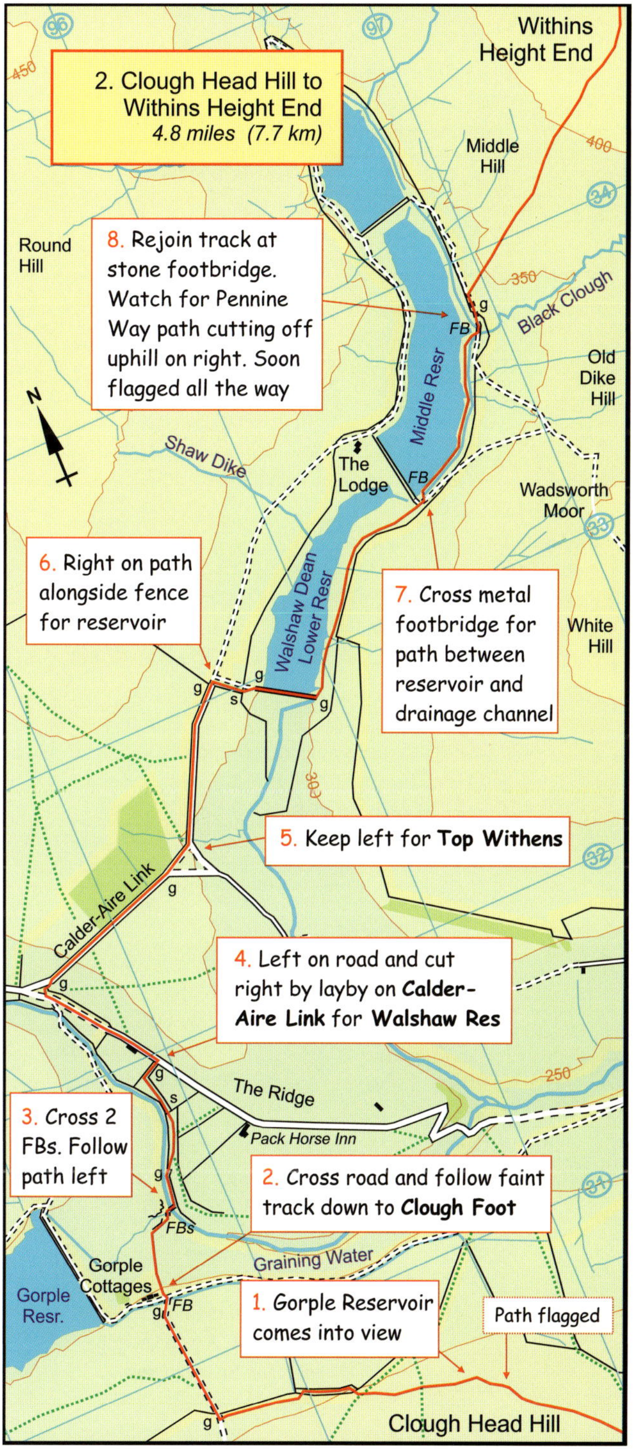

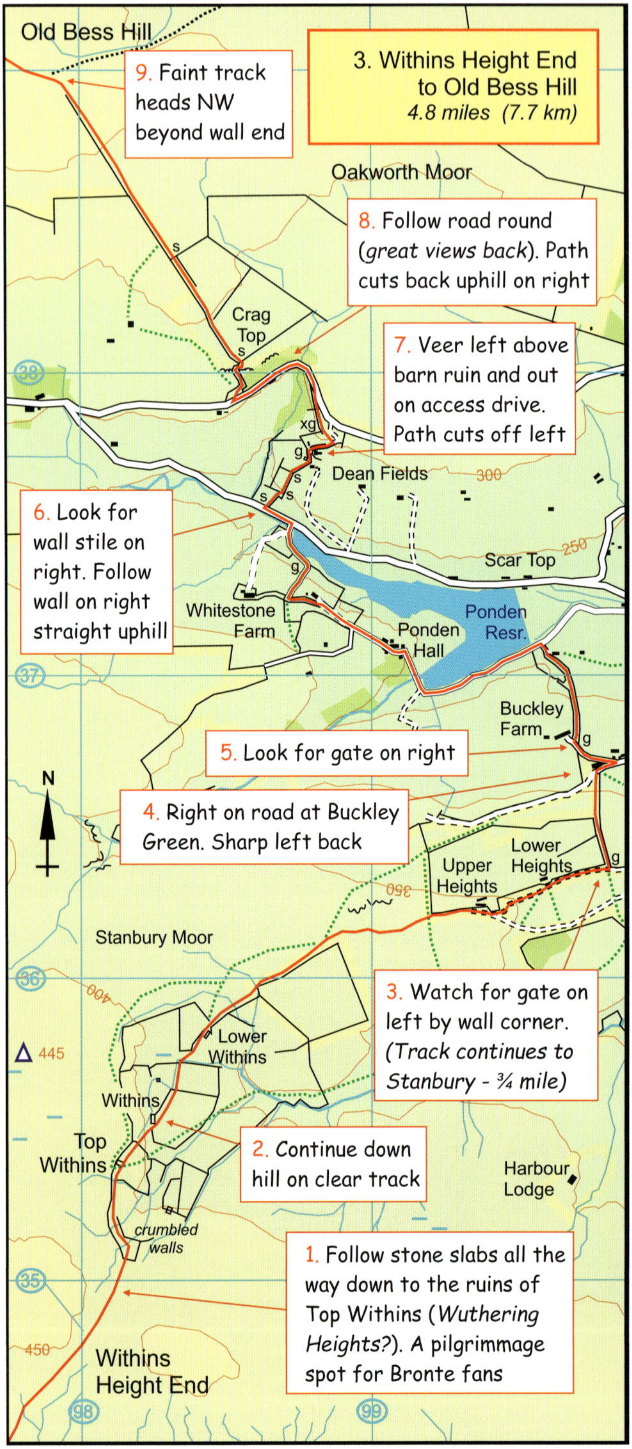

Once over the hill brow the windswept ruin of *Top Withins* comes into view. Abandoned sometime in the 1920s, its location (though not the building) is believed to be the inspiration for Emily Bronte's *Wuthering Heights*. It's a popular spot for Bronte fans, many from as far away as Japan.

The path descends northeast, with good long views ahead to Haworth. The option of taking a path to **Bronte Falls** and then on along the Bronte Way to Haworth soon presents itself (3½ miles).

Keep left past Upper Heights Farm and just past Lower Heights the Pennine Way turns sharp left at a wall corner (continue straight along the track for Stanbury – ¾ mile).

A little careful navigation brings you down to Ponden Reservoir and soon after to Ponden Hall, the more obvious inspiration for Thrushcroft Grange in *Wuthering Heights*.

Ponden Hall

The path continues above the reservoir, crossing the River Worth onto a road at the water's end. Turn left and take a wall stile on the right, climbing straight uphill and out behind a house onto a road which curves left above Dean Clough, with good views back across the reservoir.

The Pennine Way cuts back up a curving track on the right and climbs north-west onto Old Bess Hill.

Beyond a wall end the path is faint crossing the bleak, open moor and care must be taken in mist. The path eventually turns north, occasional slab paving giving confidence.

Over Cat Stone Hill a rocky meandering track begins to descend towards a stone shooting hut. Beyond this the path crosses rough, boggy ground, following a wall line and passing an array of wooden shooters' huts (called *Cowlings*).

Eventually a metal gate leads sharply left downhill, past ruins to cross the beck at Nigher Dean Hole, climbing again to join a track which curves sharply north above a waterfall at Lumb Head Beck. The path heads downhill past Lower Summer House, with the Wainman's Pinacle prominent on the horizon to the east. Cross the busy A6068, past the bus shelter and down to Ickornshaw village. Accommodation may be sought at Cowling.

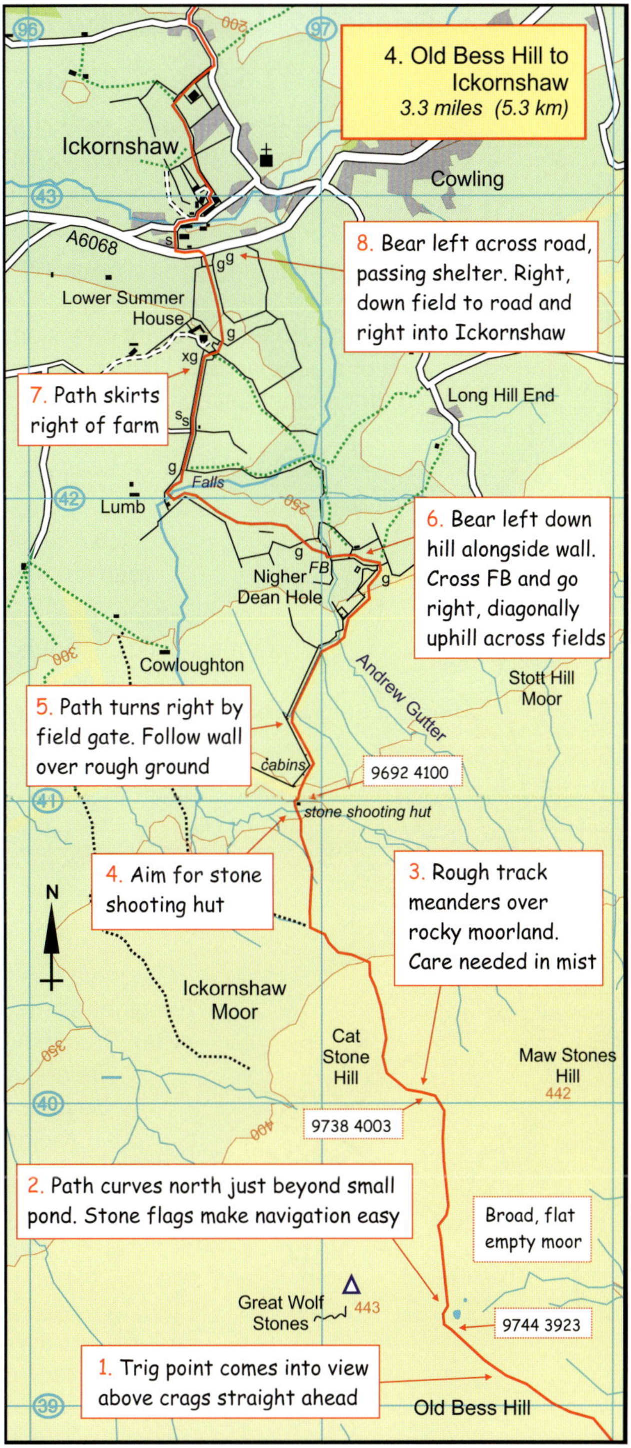

Section 2: **Ickornshaw to Malham**

17.5 miles (28.1 km)

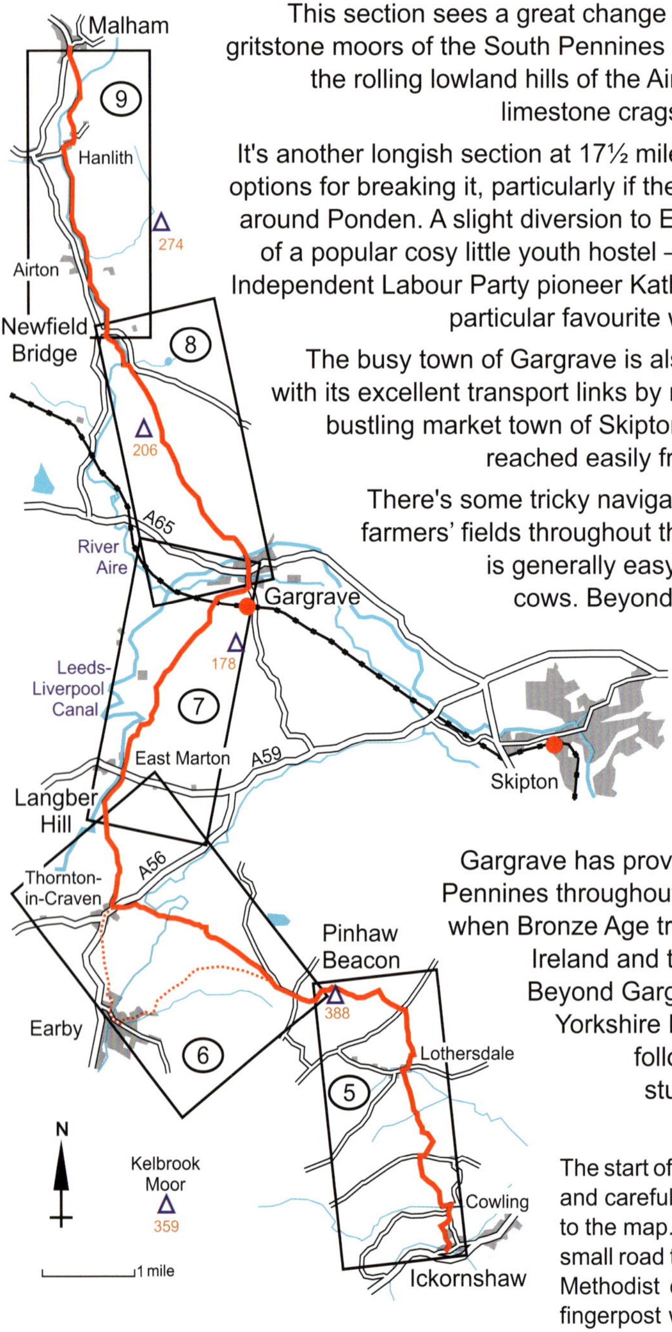

This section sees a great change in the landscape, as the gritstone moors of the South Pennines are finally left behind for the rolling lowland hills of the Aire Gap and the stunning limestone crags of the Yorkshire Dales.

It's another longish section at 17½ miles, but there are several options for breaking it, particularly if the last overnight stay was around Ponden. A slight diversion to Earby offers the prospect of a popular cosy little youth hostel – the former home of the Independent Labour Party pioneer Katherine Bruce Glasier – a particular favourite with Pennine Wayfarers.

The busy town of Gargrave is also a good spot to break, with its excellent transport links by rail, road and canal. The bustling market town of Skipton is close by and can be reached easily from here by train or bus.

There's some tricky navigation involved in crossing farmers' fields throughout the section, but the going is generally easy. Expect to meet a lot of cows. Beyond Thornton-in-Craven the moors give way to the more verdant green fields of limestone country, though here it's generally hidden beneath glacial boulder clay. The Aire Gap at Gargrave has provided a route through the Pennines throughout history and pre-history, when Bronze Age traders travelled between Ireland and the European Continent. Beyond Gargrave the way enters the Yorkshire Dales National Park and follows the River Aire to the stunning limestone cliffs at Malham Cove.

The start of this section is rather finicky and careful attention needs to be paid to the map. From Ickornhsaw take the small road that rises behind the former Methodist chapel and look for a **PW** fingerpost which points the way north across fields, eventually crossing right through a yard to join **Gill Lane**. At a left bend a narrow lane is followed steeply down to the right, across Gill Bridge and left along the access track to a house.

The way now climbs north again across fields, passing Low and High Stubbing Farms to reach **Cowling Hill Lane**. A right and left lead downhill and at a sharp right a stile leads ahead down fields for **Lothersdale**. Cross the beck and climb again, passing through Woodhead Farm yard and out along the access road. Lothersdale, with its prominent chimney, nestles deeply down in the valley to the right and is the last of the South Pennine mill towns along the route.

From Lothersdale, the way continues climbing north across more fields, past Hewitts Farm and out onto open moor to reach the highest point of the day at Pinhaw Beacon.

Lothersdale

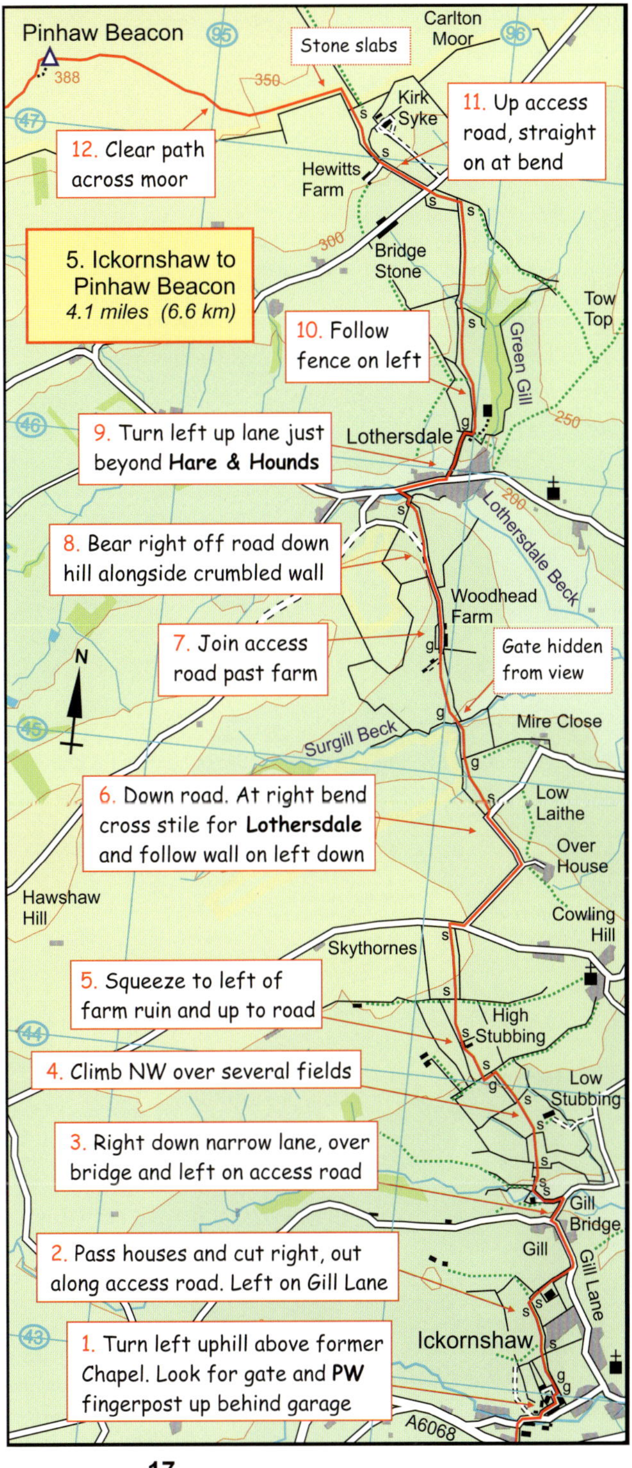

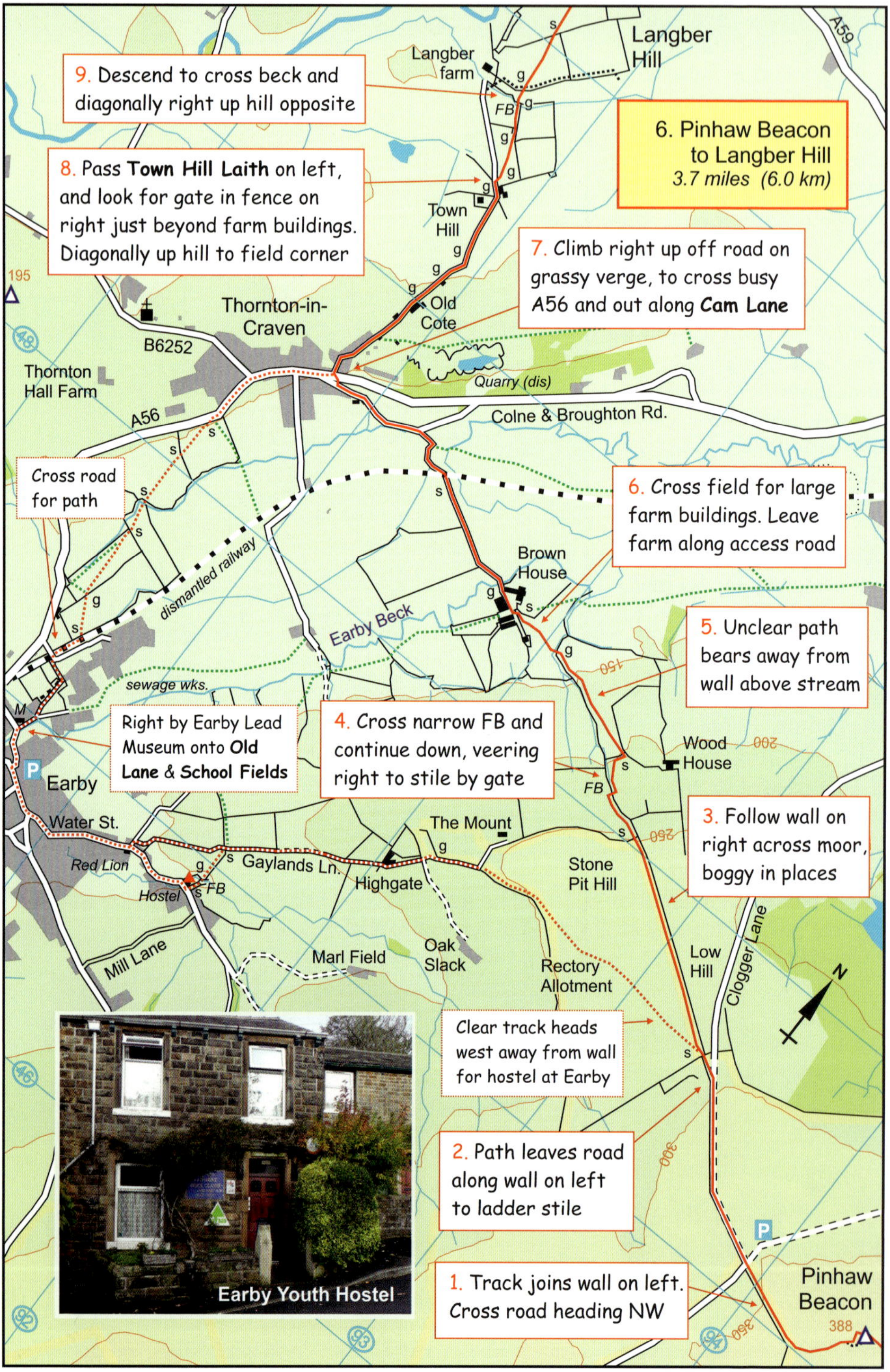
6. Pinhaw Beacon
to Langber Hill
3.7 miles (6.0 km)
1. Track joins wall on left. Cross road heading NW
2. Path leaves road along wall on left to ladder stile
Clear track heads west away from wall for hostel at Earby
3. Follow wall on right across moor, boggy in places
4. Cross narrow FB and continue down, veering right to stile by gate
5. Unclear path bears away from wall above stream
6. Cross field for large farm buildings. Leave farm along access road
7. Climb right up off road on grassy verge, to cross busy A56 and out along Cam Lane
8. Pass Town Hill Laith on left, and look for gate in fence on right just beyond farm buildings. Diagonally up hill to field corner
9. Descend to cross beck and diagonally right up hill opposite
Cross road for path
Right by Earby Lead Museum onto Old Lane & School Fields
Langber Hill
Langber farm
Town Hill
Old Cote
Thornton-in-Craven
B6252
Thornton Hall Farm
A56
A59
Quarry (dis)
Colne & Broughton Rd.
dismantled railway
Earby Beck
Brown House
Wood House
sewage wks.
Earby
Water St.
Red Lion
Hostel
Gaylands Ln.
Highgate
The Mount
Stone Pit Hill
Mill Lane
Marl Field
Oak Slack
Rectory Allotment
Low Hill
Clogger Lane
Pinhaw Beacon
388
195
Earby Youth Hostel

From the trig point the path heads SW to join a wall, then NW to cross **Skipton Old Road** and along **Clogger Lane**, eventually cutting left alongside a wall to a ladderstile. Beyond this the path forks, left for Earby and its popular youth hostel, or straight on for **Thornton-in-Craven**.

Across the busy A56 the Pennine Way follows **Cam Lane** and just beyond farm buildings at Town Hill a stile leads NNW across fields to Langber Hill, before dropping to join the Leeds-Liverpool canal, passing East Marton and the famous double-arched bridge carrying the A59.

The 127-mile canal is the longest in England, with 91 locks and a mile-long tunnel. It was completed in 1816, some 51 years after it was first proposed.

The canal can be followed all the way to Gargrave, (adding 1¼ miles), though the Pennine Way cuts off at Bridge 162 to head NE across fields, guided on the final stretch by the prominent tower of St. Andrew's Church.

Road bridge across the canal at East Marton

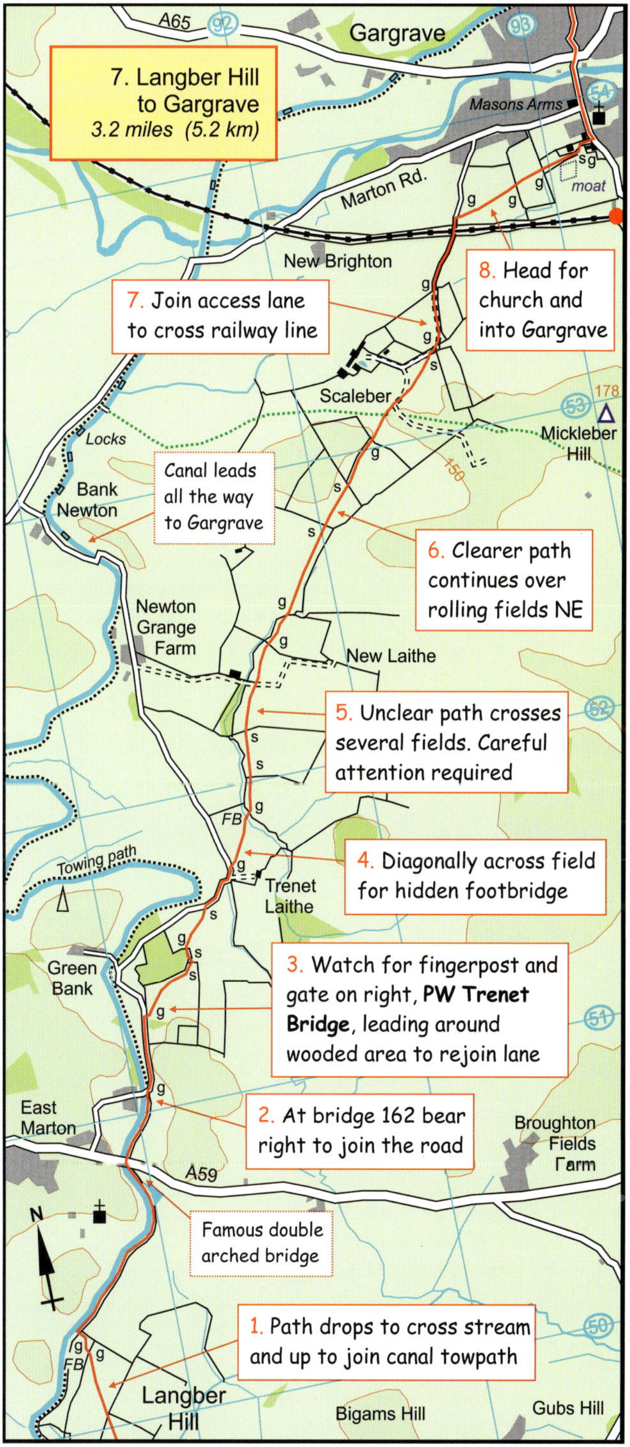

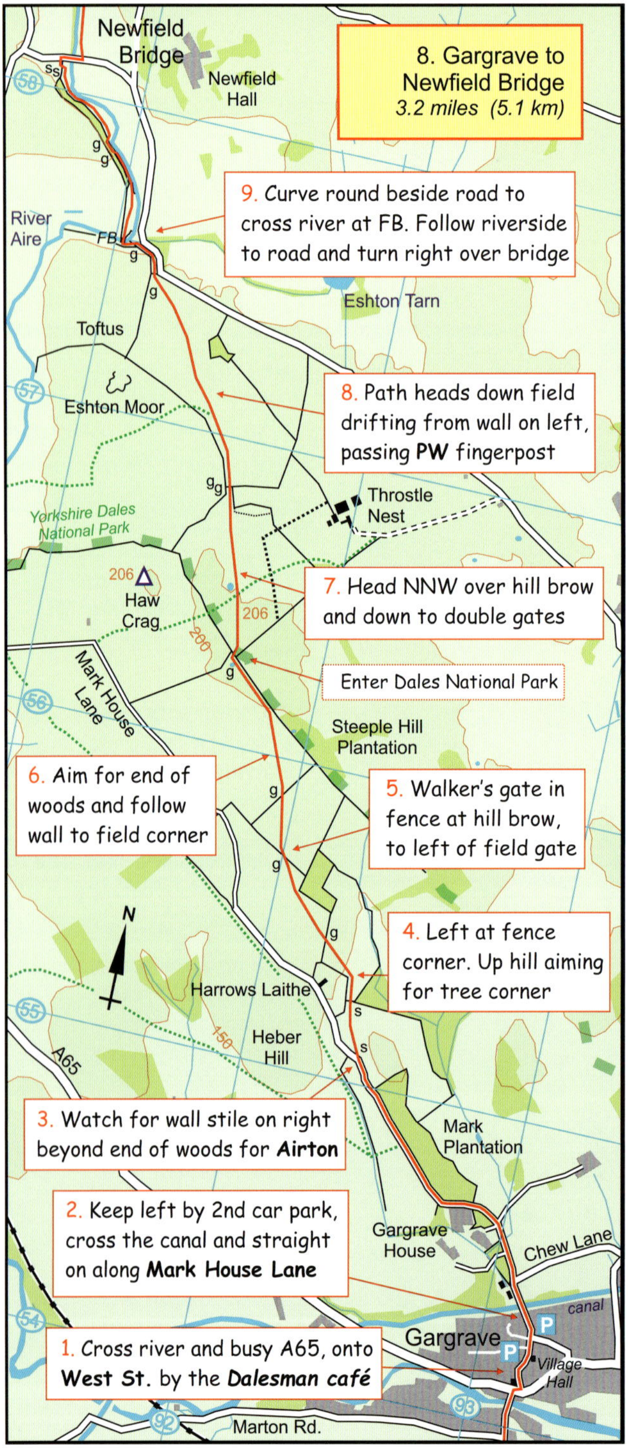

Gargrave is a great place to break the journey, with plenty of shops, facilties and accommodation, and good transport links with the railway station on the Leeds-Carlisle line and bus links to nearby Skipton. It is also the last real chance to stock up before Hawes. Even if you're just passing through, the popular *Dalesman café* is bound to attract.

From the main A65 pass the café along **West St**, keeping left past the second car park to cross the canal and on along **Mark House Lane**.

At the end of some woods on the right, a hidden wall stile leads NW climbing across fields to enter the *Yorkshire Dales National Park*. A little care is needed following the path over the green fields of Eshton Moor and down to join the River Aire, which is now followed all the way to Malham.

It's an easy, lazy, riverside ramble, though it can be muddy in places after rain.

At Newfield Bridge the path crosses to the eastern bank. The villages of Airton and Kirkby Malham can be visted by crossing the river, otherwise you soon arrive at the tiny village of Hanlith. Hanlith Manor is mentioned in the Domesday Book. The present hall dates from the 17th century, but was largely rebuilt in the early 20th century.

The path climbs up through Hanlith, before continuing north through fields, high above the river. Malham Cove soon comes tantalisingly into view, before the path drops down to rejoin the river near Aire Head, where the river's waters emerge from underground limestone chambers.

Just before entering Malham, a popular path for **Janet's Foss** cuts off to the right, leading on to Gordale Scar – one of Wainwright's offroute highlights of the Pennine Way, and well worth a visit if time permits.

Approaching Malham

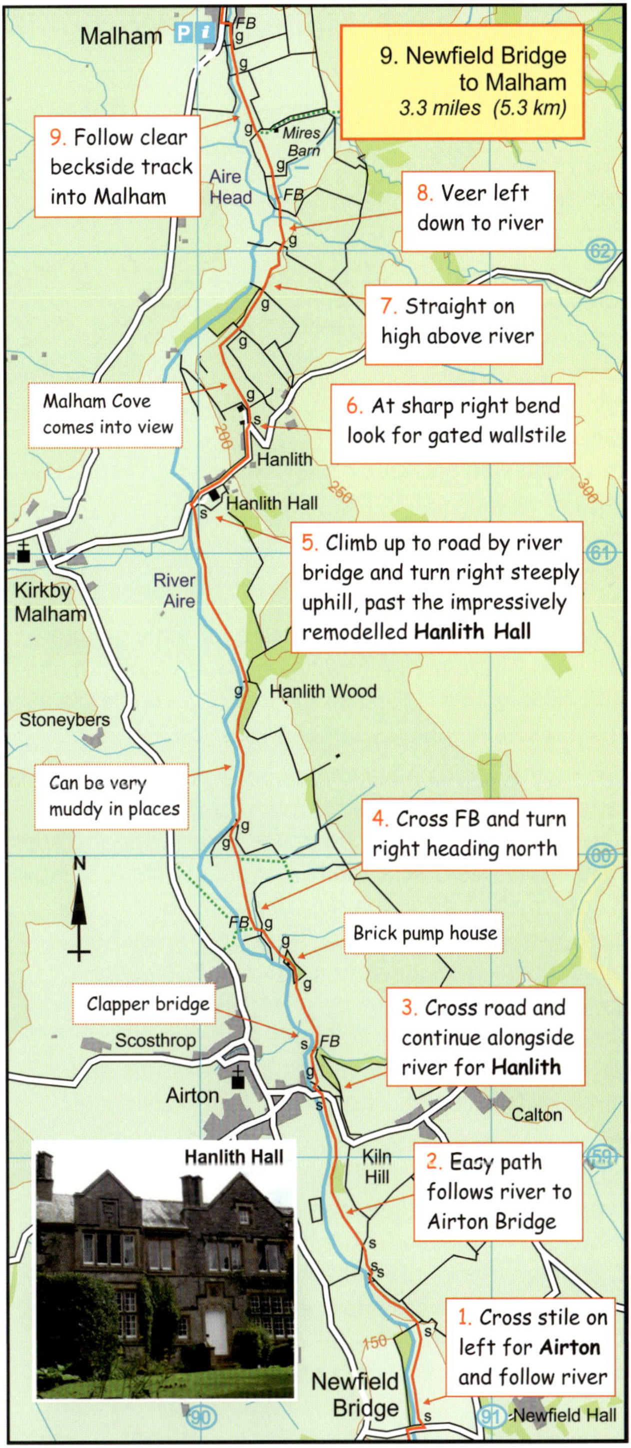

Section 3: **Malham to Horton-in-Ribblesdale**

14.8 miles (*23.8 km*)

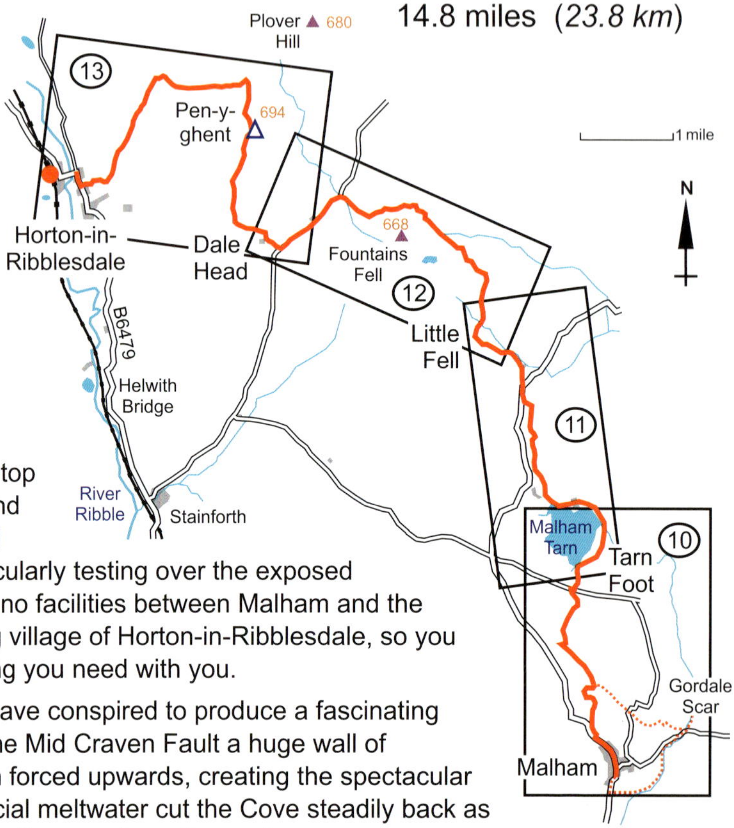

This section is one of the highlights of the Pennine Way.

At 15 miles with two mountains to cross it can be tough going, but given a fine sunny day you will be rewarded with superb views, especially from the top of Pen-y-ghent. Wind and rain though will make the trek particularly testing over the exposed fell tops. There are no facilities between Malham and the gritty little quarrying village of Horton-in-Ribblesdale, so you must take everything you need with you.

Geological forces have conspired to produce a fascinating landscape. Along the Mid Craven Fault a huge wall of limestone has been forced upwards, creating the spectacular Malham Cove. Glacial meltwater cut the Cove steadily back as it once rushed down the now dry valley and cascaded over the lip. The Great Scar limestone – almost pure calcium carbonate - has been eaten away over the millennia by weakly acidic rainwater, creating the intricately sculptured limestone pavements, and below ground deep caverns and tunnels. This is potholing country par excellence.

Beyond Malham Tarn, which sits on an upraised slab of impervious ancient bedrock, Yordale shales topped with a hard gritstone cap form the two peaks that must be crossed. Fountains Fell, named by the Cistercian monks of Fountains Abbey who owned this land, is a typically domed Pennine moorland peak, but Pen-y-ghent – *hill of the winds* – is a real, if humble, mountain with a steep rocky western face and distinctive stepped profile.

Pinnacle, Pen-y-ghent

Malham Cove

The Three Peaks, with Pen-y-ghent prominent, seen from Fountains Fell

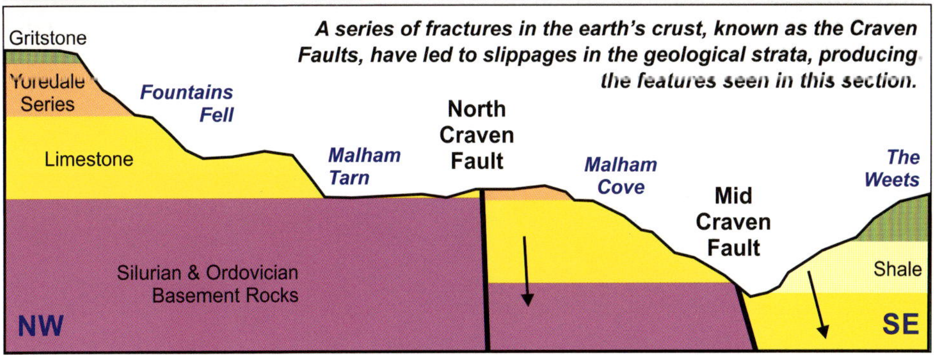

A series of fractures in the earth's crust, known as the Craven Faults, have led to slippages in the geological strata, producing the features seen in this section.

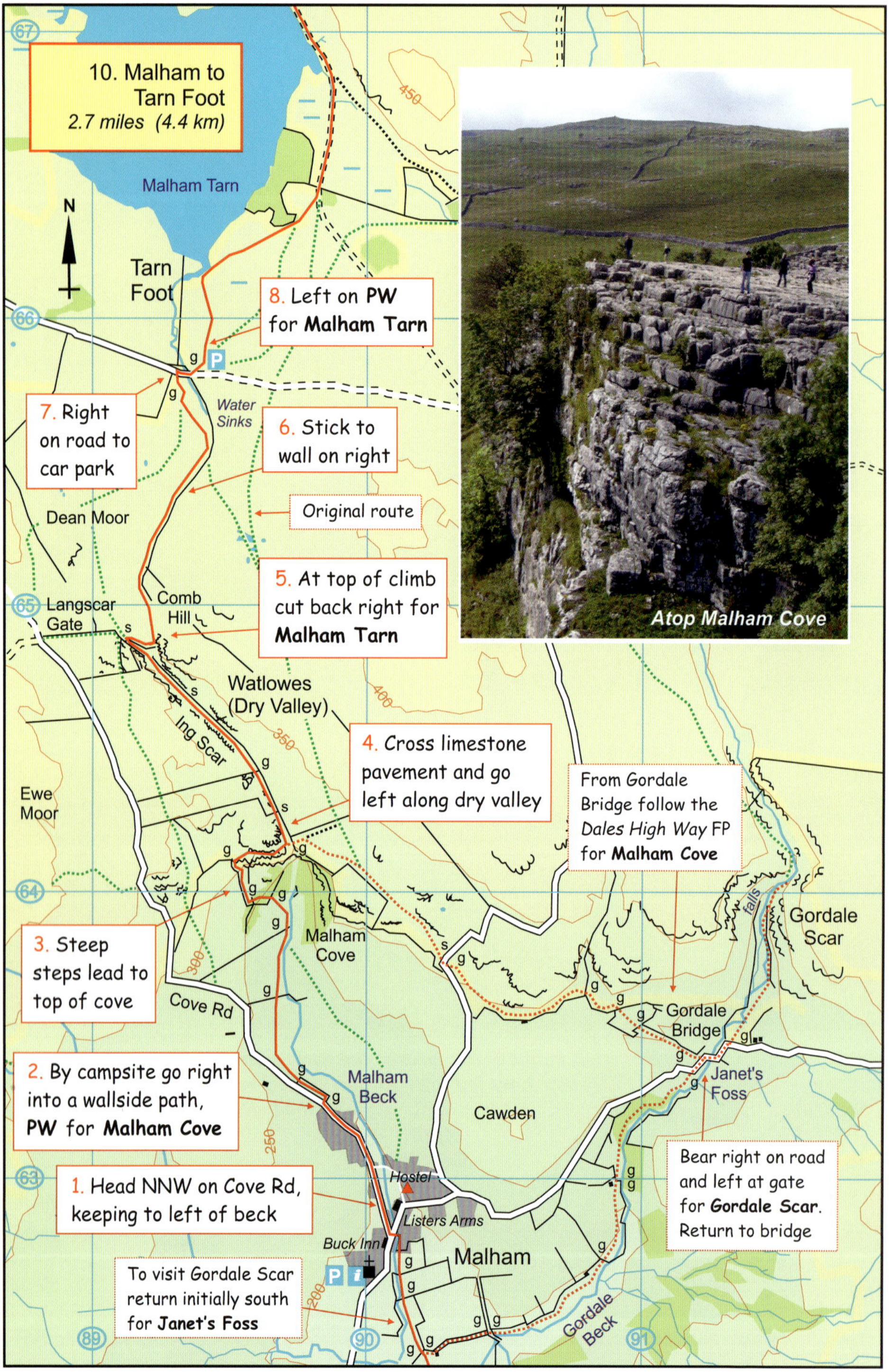
10. Malham to Tarn Foot
2.7 miles (4.4 km)
Malham Tarn
N
Tarn Foot
8. Left on PW for Malham Tarn
P
7. Right on road to car park
Water Sinks
6. Stick to wall on right
Original route
Dean Moor
5. At top of climb cut back right for Malham Tarn
Langscar Gate
Comb Hill
Watlowes (Dry Valley)
Ing Scar
4. Cross limestone pavement and go left along dry valley
From Gordale Bridge follow the Dales High Way FP for Malham Cove
Ewe Moor
Gordale Scar
falls
Malham Cove
3. Steep steps lead to top of cove
Cove Rd
Gordale Bridge
Janet's Foss
2. By campsite go right into a wallside path, PW for Malham Cove
Malham Beck
Cawden
Bear right on road and left at gate for Gordale Scar. Return to bridge
1. Head NNW on Cove Rd, keeping to left of beck
Hostel
Listers Arms
Buck Inn
Malham
To visit Gordale Scar return initially south for Janet's Foss
Gordale Beck
Atop Malham Cove

Leave Malham heading north along the **Cove Road**. Just beyond Town Head Farm a gate on the right takes the **Pennine Way** towards the impressive 80-metre high cliffs of **Malham Cove**.

Stone steps on the left lead from the foot of the Cove steeply upwards. Cross the limestone pavement on top carefully, stepping between each ridge (called *clints*), avoiding the deep gaps (called *grykes*). By the wall turn left along the dry valley of Watlowes. After a steep rocky climb at the northern end, turn back sharp right, around Comb Hill and continue NNE, passing Water Sinks where the young waters of the River Aire disappear underground, to reappear just south of Malham.

Cross the road and continue north to **Malham Tarn** – the highest natural lake in England. The Pennine Way follows a track around the eastern side to Malham Tarn House, run as a field studies centre. Pass behind the house and out along the access road. Just before a house on the right, a gate leads north across fields for **Tennant Gill**. Cross a road and head up the access track to Tennant Gill Farm, skirting to the left and uphill to a wall stile. Cross and swing left, then right, climbing alongside a crumbled wall to Little Fell.

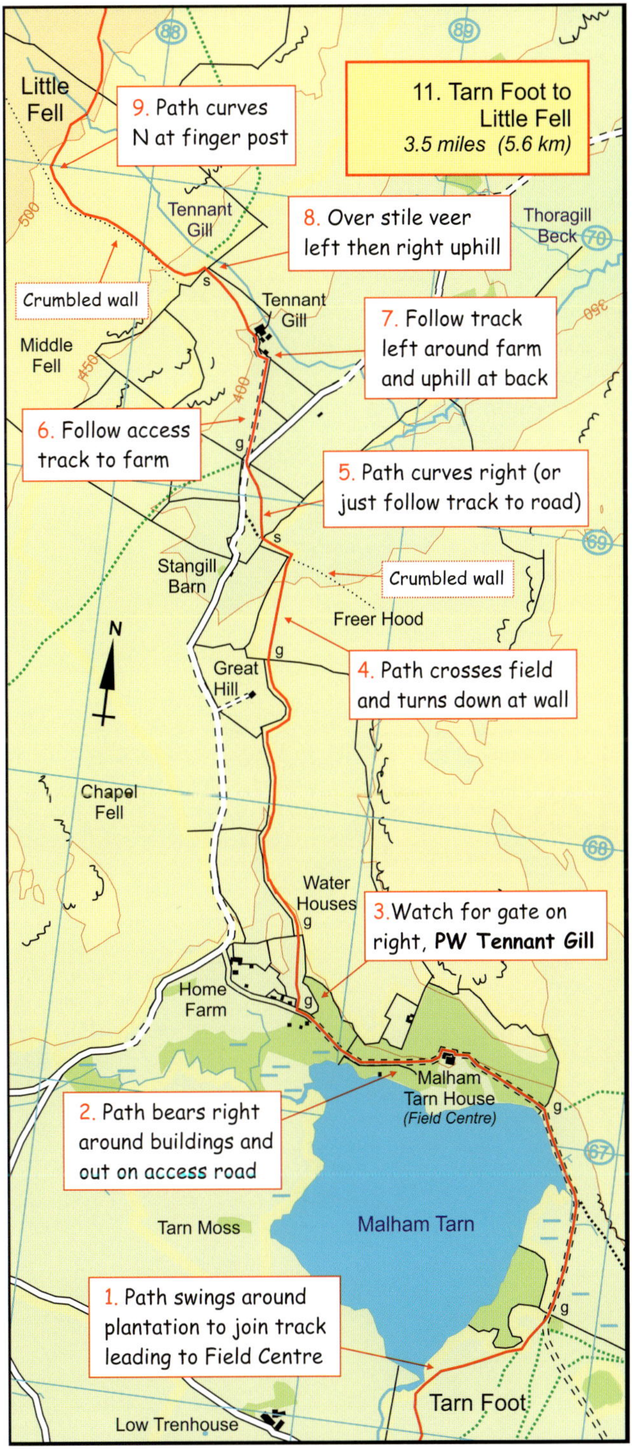

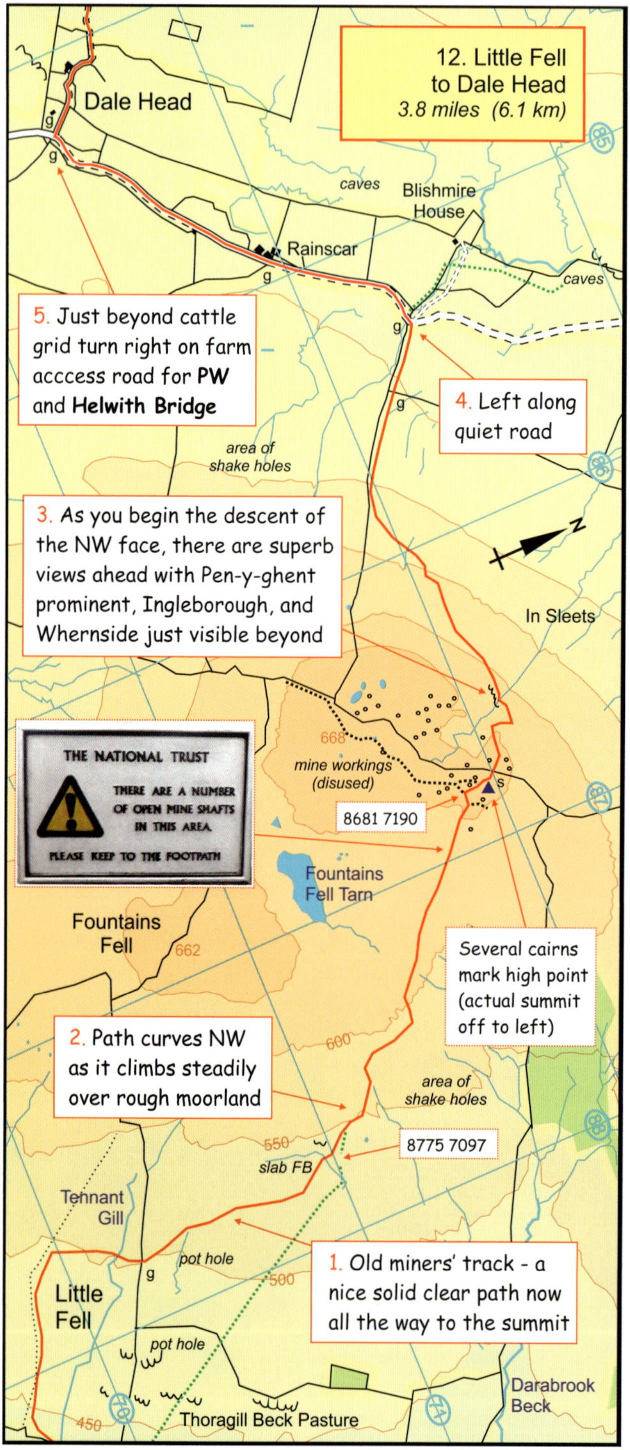

A fingerpost marks a right turn along an old miners' track, heading north, This good track curves gradually NW, climbing to skirt the summit of Fountains Fell to the right. The top is pockmarked with old coal mine shafts, worked mainly in the early 19th century. Even in mist route finding here is not too difficult.

The path now descends the north western face of the fell, with great views ahead of the Yorkshire Three Peaks. Pen-y-ghent is dominant, with Ingleborough behind to the left and Whernside peeking over to the right.

Turn left along the road for just under a mile, and right for **Helwith Bridge**, passing through the yard of Dale Head Farm. A track leads WNW to the deep sinkhole of Churn Milk Hole, where it cuts right for **Pen-y-ghent**, which is now showing its finest profile.

The climb to the summit looks steep and finishes with a mini-scramble, but you're very quickly up to relax at the summit shelter.

The descent is long, but clear and easy, heading from the trig point initially northwards, along the rim, then downhill westwards. If time permits short diversions will lead you to the striking potholes Hunt Pot and Hull Pot. Finally a rocky enclosed lane leads SE down to the village.

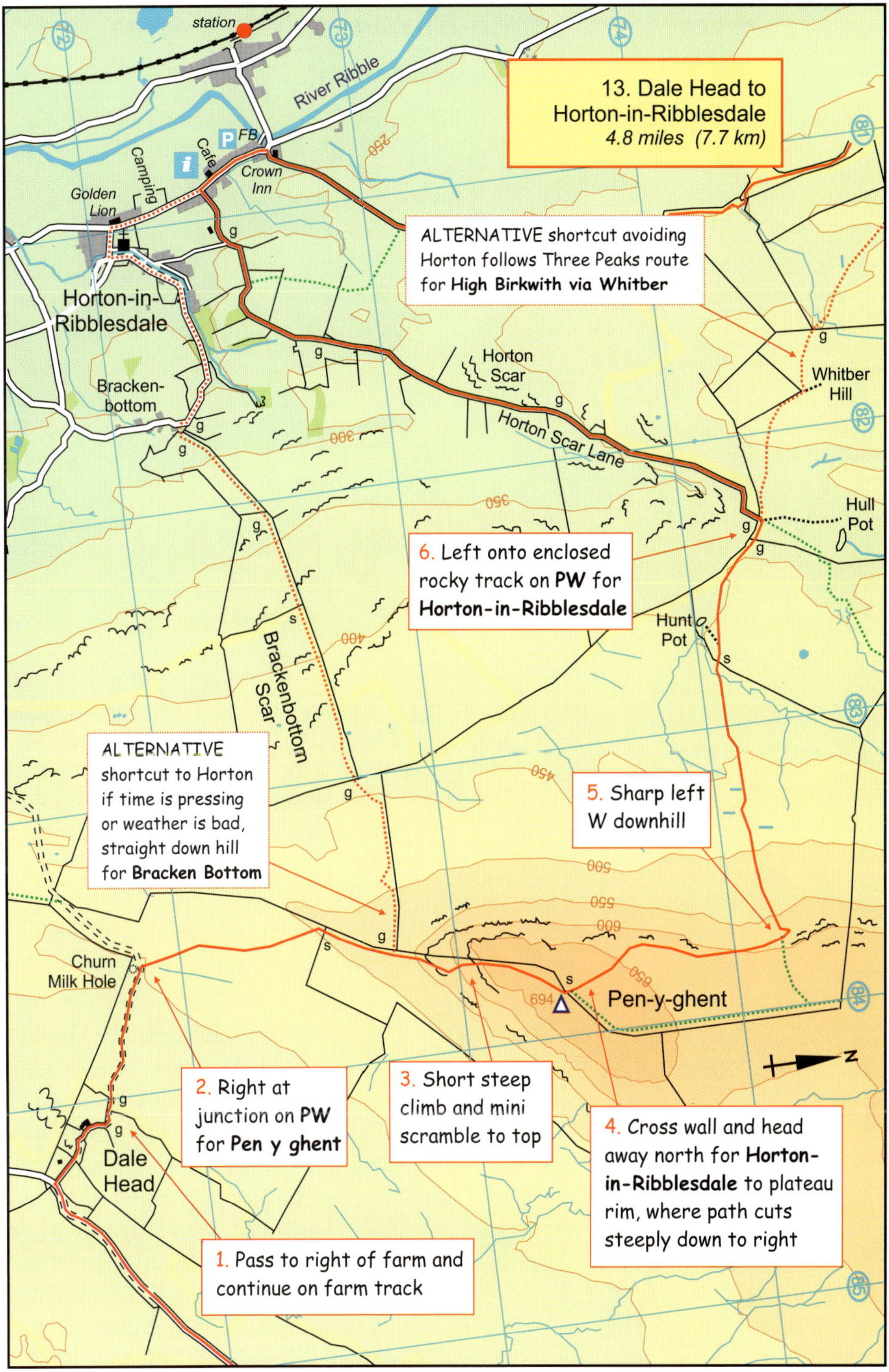
13. Dale Head to Horton-in-Ribblesdale
4.8 miles (7.7 km)
station
River Ribble
FB
Cafe
Crown Inn
Camping
Golden Lion
Horton-in-Ribblesdale
Bracken-bottom
ALTERNATIVE shortcut avoiding Horton follows Three Peaks route for **High Birkwith via Whitber**
Horton Scar
Horton Scar Lane
Whitber Hill
Hull Pot
Hunt Pot
6. Left onto enclosed rocky track on **PW** for **Horton-in-Ribblesdale**
Brackenbottom Scar
ALTERNATIVE shortcut to Horton if time is pressing or weather is bad, straight down hill for **Bracken Bottom**
5. Sharp left W downhill
Churn Milk Hole
Pen-y-ghent
694
Dale Head
2. Right at junction on **PW** for **Pen y ghent**
3. Short steep climb and mini scramble to top
4. Cross wall and head away north for **Horton-in-Ribblesdale** to plateau rim, where path cuts steeply down to right
1. Pass to right of farm and continue on farm track
N

Section 4: **Horton-in-Ribblesdale to Hawes**

13.6 miles (*21.9 km*)

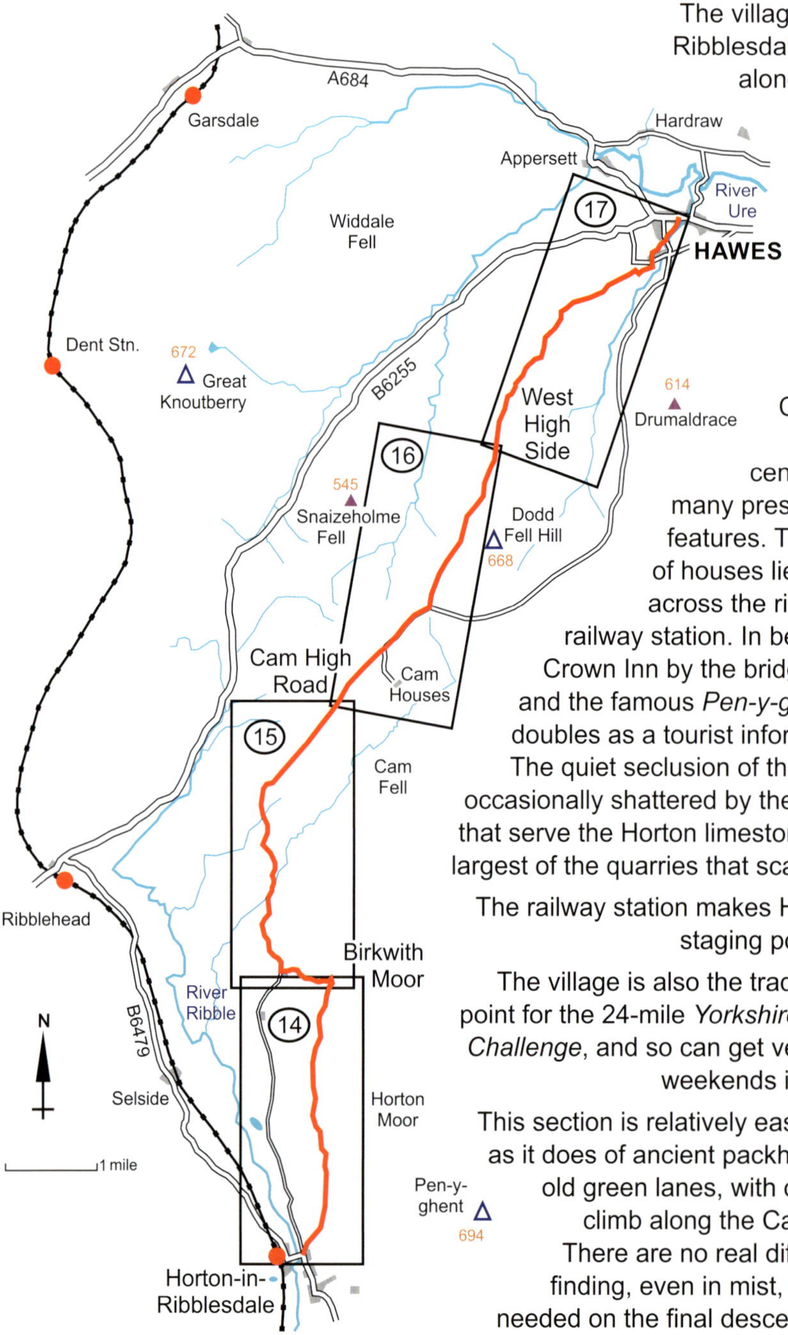

The village of Horton-in-Ribblesdale is strung out along half a mile of the B6479. A cluster of houses lie to the south, around the Golden Lion Hotel and the iconic St Oswald's Church, with its square 16th century tower and many preserved Norman features. The main group of houses lies to the north, across the river around the railway station. In between are the Crown Inn by the bridge, a campsite and the famous *Pen-y-ghent Café* that doubles as a tourist information centre. The quiet seclusion of the settlement is occasionally shattered by the roar of lorries that serve the Horton limestone quarry - the largest of the quarries that scar Ribblesdale.

The railway station makes Horton a useful staging post on the trail.

The village is also the traditional starting point for the 24-mile *Yorkshire Three Peaks Challenge*, and so can get very crowded at weekends in the summer.

This section is relatively easy, making use as it does of ancient packhorse trails and old green lanes, with only one major climb along the Cam High Road. There are no real difficulties route-finding, even in mist, though care is needed on the final descent into Hawes.

The Crown Inn, Horton-in-Ribblesdale

From the back of the Crown Inn car park the **Pennine Way** follows a walled track rising NE for **Birkwith Moor**. The green lane, once used by the monks of Jervaulx Abbey who bred horses here, climbs steadily, curving north and levelling out at Sell Gill Holes. This marks the top of the Great Scar Limestone and the route is peppered with pot holes and shake holes.

There are glorious views across and back down the valley, with the huge scar of Horton Quarry now clearly visible. The distinctive flat top of Ingleborough can be seen peeking above Simon Fell, and to the north Whernside rears up above the distictive Ribblehead Viaduct.

The way is easy to follow until Birkwith Moor, where the path cuts off left from the more obvious track beyond a gate.

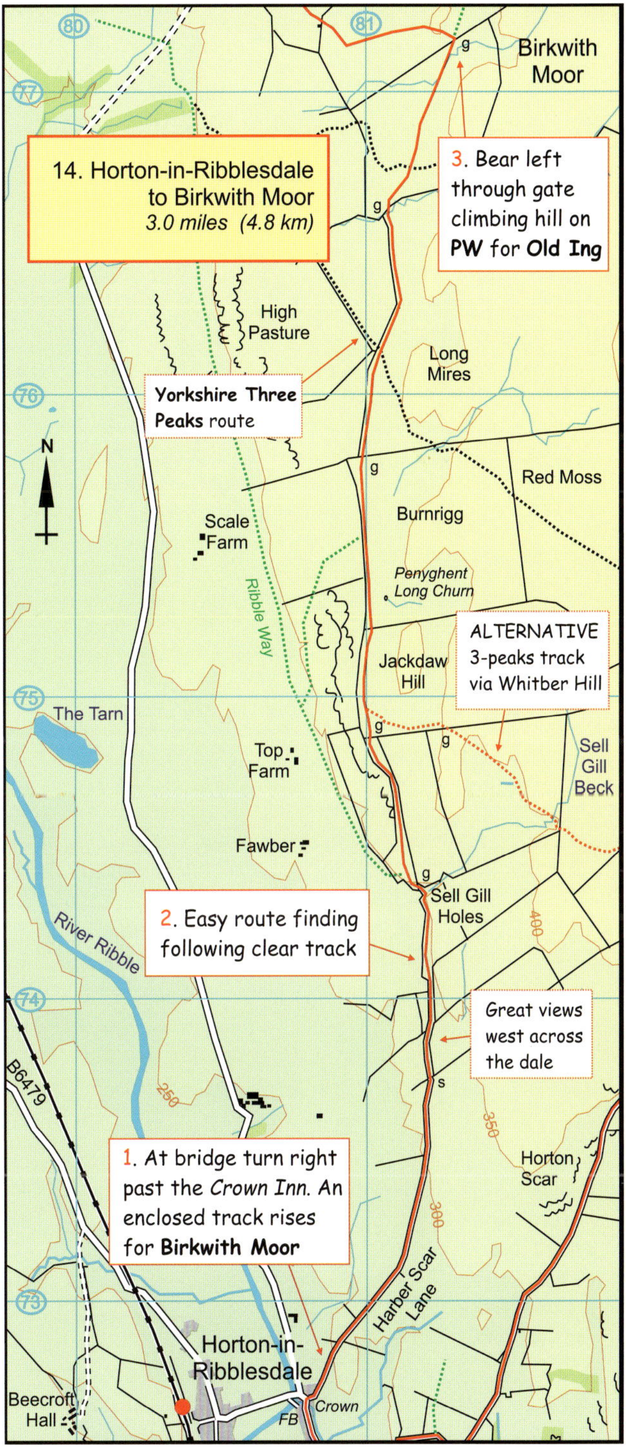

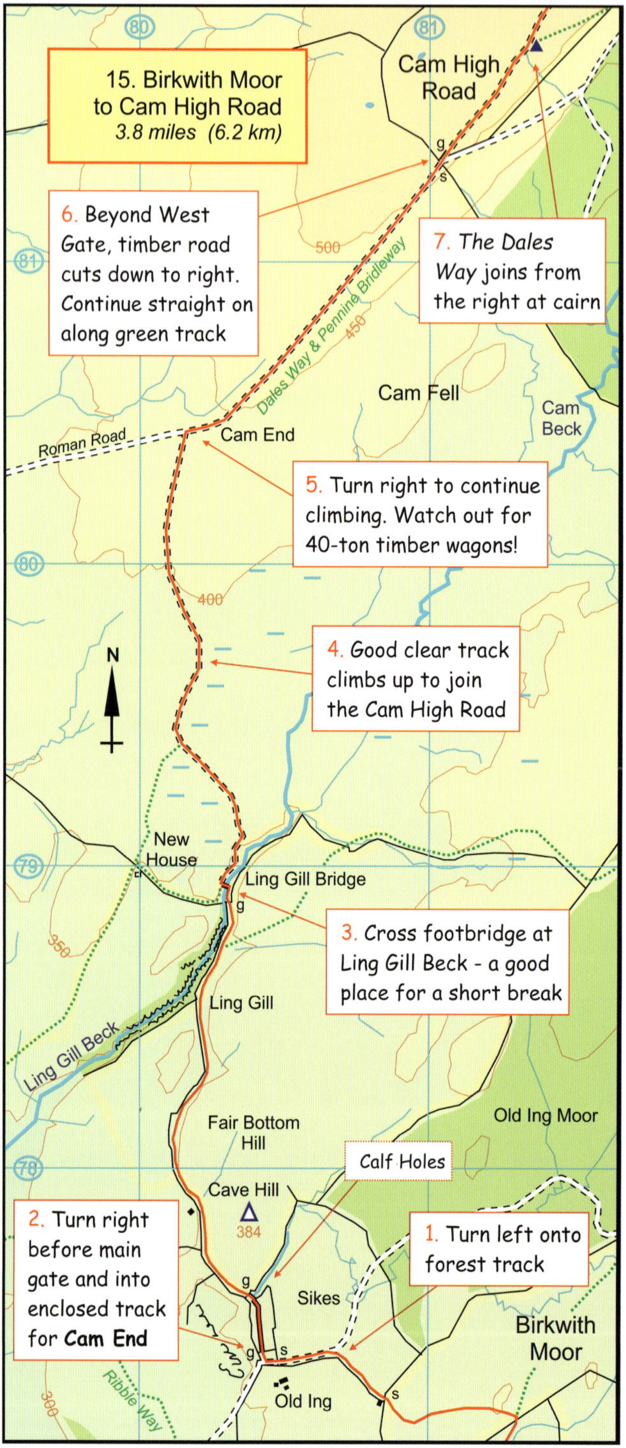

A clear path heads west over a hill brow and down by a barn, following a wall on the left to join a forest track past the farm at Old Ing. A right turn before the main gate for **Cam End** takes you past the pothole (over the wall) at Calf Holes, which is a good spot for a break.

Ling Gill Bridge

Otherwise continue following the wall on the left to the deep wooded gorge at **Ling Gill** – now a National Nature Reserve. Cross the stone bridge, with its faded inscription: *Anno 1765. This bridge was repaired at the charge of the whole West Rideing.*

A good track now leads up to join the **Cam High Road**, an old Roman road that

Timber trucks on Cam High Road

leads from Ingleton, via Ribblehead, over Cam Fell and on to the fort at Bainbridge in Wensleydale. It became a major turnpike road in late 18th century before the construction of the modern road along Widdale to Hawes. More recently it has been resurfaced to carry 40-tonne timber trucks bringing logs down from Cam and Greenfield forests. The road is also shared with the **Pennine Bridleway** and **Dales Way**.

Beyond West Gate the modern forest road cuts down to the right, the Pennine Way continuing NE along a much more pleasant green lane. The Dales Way takes its leave for Cam Houses by a large cairn, with the Pennine Bridleway departing at Cold Keld Gate for Newby Head. The way here is now level and on tarmac, but a little further on the trail takes a left turn at Kidhow Gate to join a track - **West Cam Road** – which heads NE for Hawes to skirt the western flank of Dodd Fell.

The deep narrow valley of Snaizeholme opens down to the left.

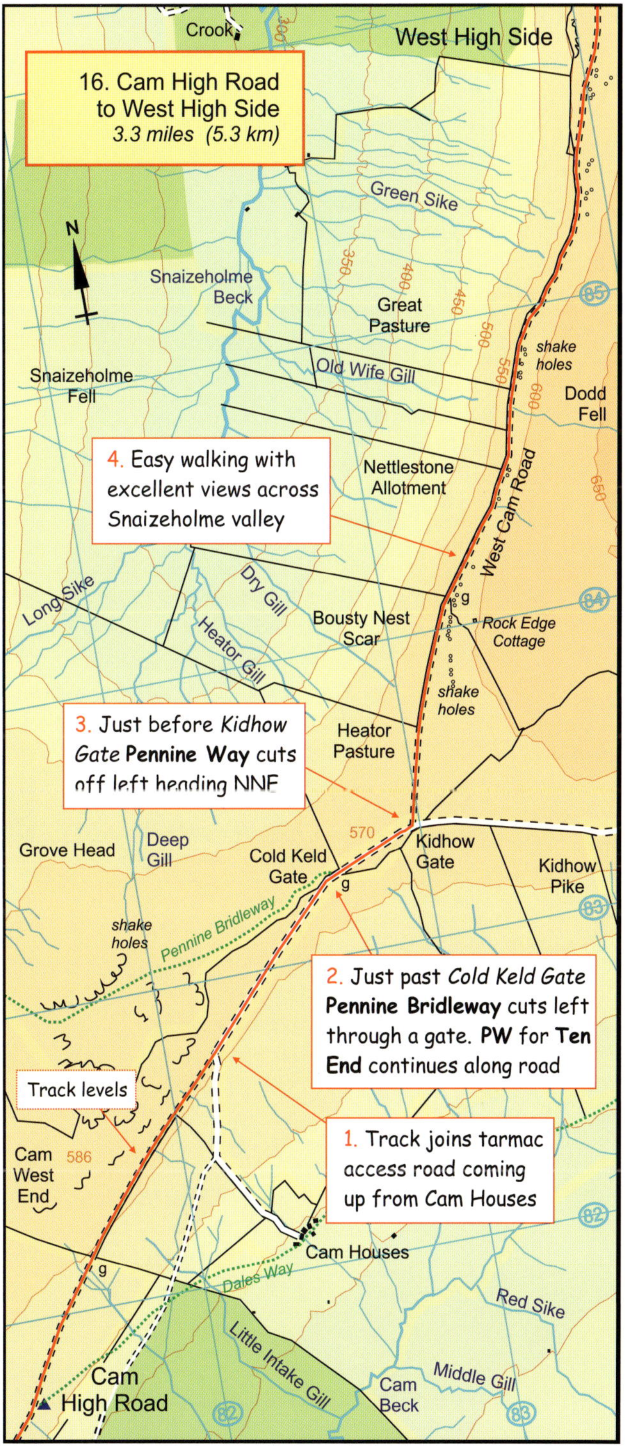

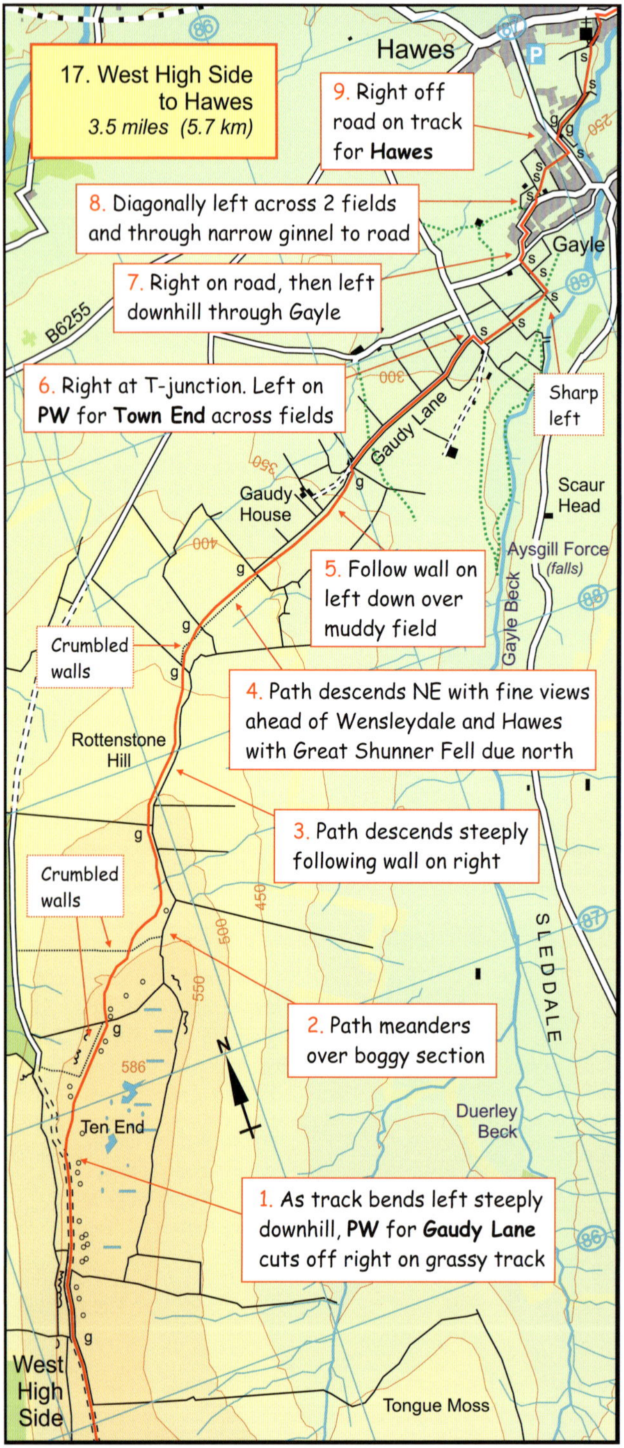

The **Pennine Way** leaves the track for **Gaudy Lane** at Ten End, and the path now becomes indistinct in places, so care is needed. Beyond a gate the path meanders over boggy ground as it begins to descend, but eventually picks up a wall on the right over Rottenstone Hill.

The broad, glacially carved valley of Wensleydale now opens out, with Hawes, *the capital of Upper Wensleydale*, prominent ahead.

The path drops to join Gaudy Lane, before cutting across fields for the jumbled houses of Gayle. A tricky route picks its way through fields and ginnels to join Gayle Beck before squeezing past St. Margaret's Church and hitting the cobbled main street of Hawes.

The market town of Hawes has everything a walker needs: a good range of accommodation including a popular youth hostel; lots of pubs and cafes, with possibly the best fish and chips in the Dales; plenty of shops, banks and other services; a traditional ropemakers, the Dales Country Museum and the famous Wensleydale Creamery. There's also a local bus link to Garsdale station on the Settle-Carlisle line which makes Hawes a perfect staging post on the Mid Pennine Way.

Upper Ribblesdale (top); by Old Ing (above); agile sheep on the Pennine Way (right); autumn on Great Shunner Fell (below).

Section 5: **Hawes to Tan Hill**

16.3 miles (*26.2 km*)

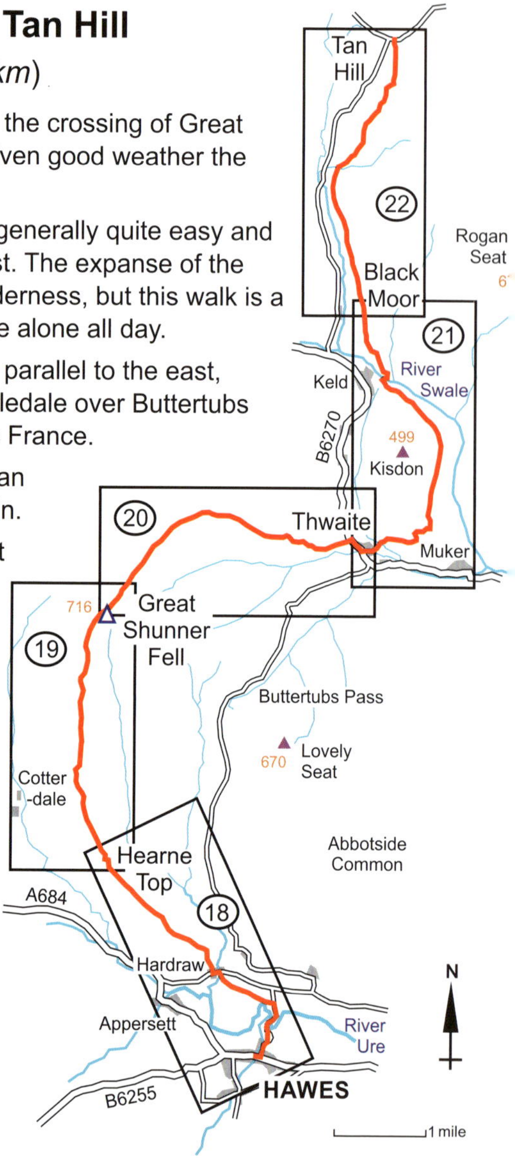

Another highlight on the Pennine Way is the crossing of Great Shunner Fell, the highest peak so far. Given good weather the views throughout are truly stunning.

The climb up is long, but the gradient is generally quite easy and route finding straightforward, even in mist. The expanse of the broad fell tops gives a true feeling of wilderness, but this walk is a popular one and so you are unlikely to be alone all day.

In 2014 the steep, narrow road that runs parallel to the east, climbing between Wensleydale and Swaledale over Buttertubs Pass, found world fame with the Tour De France.

Great Shunner Fell is exposed, so you can expect a rough trek in high winds and rain.

There are options to break this section at Thwaite, Muker or Keld, with plenty of choice of accommodation and refreshments. Muker also offers the option of a lower level, but longer riverside route to Keld. Keld is an important staging post on the *Coast to Coast* walk, so can get quite busy. The circular route between the three Swaledale villages makes a popular afternoon walk.

Leaving Thwaite

The pub at Tan Hill – the highest pub in Britain – is justifiably a Pennine Way institution and marks (almost) the half way point on the Mid Pennine Way. Booking ahead is essential.

Stock up at Hawes, as the next opportunity for provisions is Middleton-in-Teesdale.

From the centre of Hawes head down to the road junction at the eastern end of town, by the old railway station and National Park Centre. Take the road north to cross the river at Haylands Bridge, and where the road begins to climb look for a gate up in the wall on the left which leads across fields to **Hardraw**. This small hamlet offers plenty of accommodation and is an optional overnight spot beyond Hawes. To visit England's highest single drop waterfall - 30 metres - head through the pub.

An old miners' track just beside the old **School House** at the western end of Hardraw leads NW for **Thwaite** to begin the long but steady climb to Great Shunner Fell.

Beyond the intake gate the track forks left and it's hard to avoid constantly looking back at the superb views across Wensleydale.

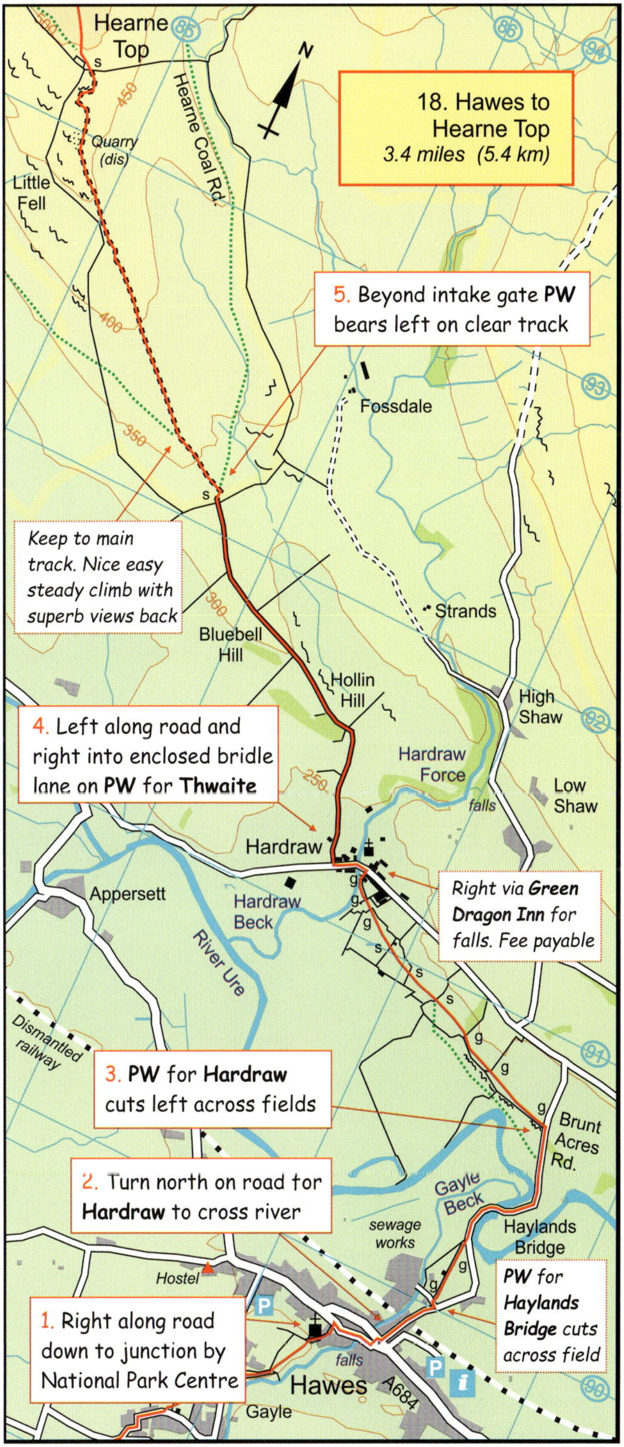

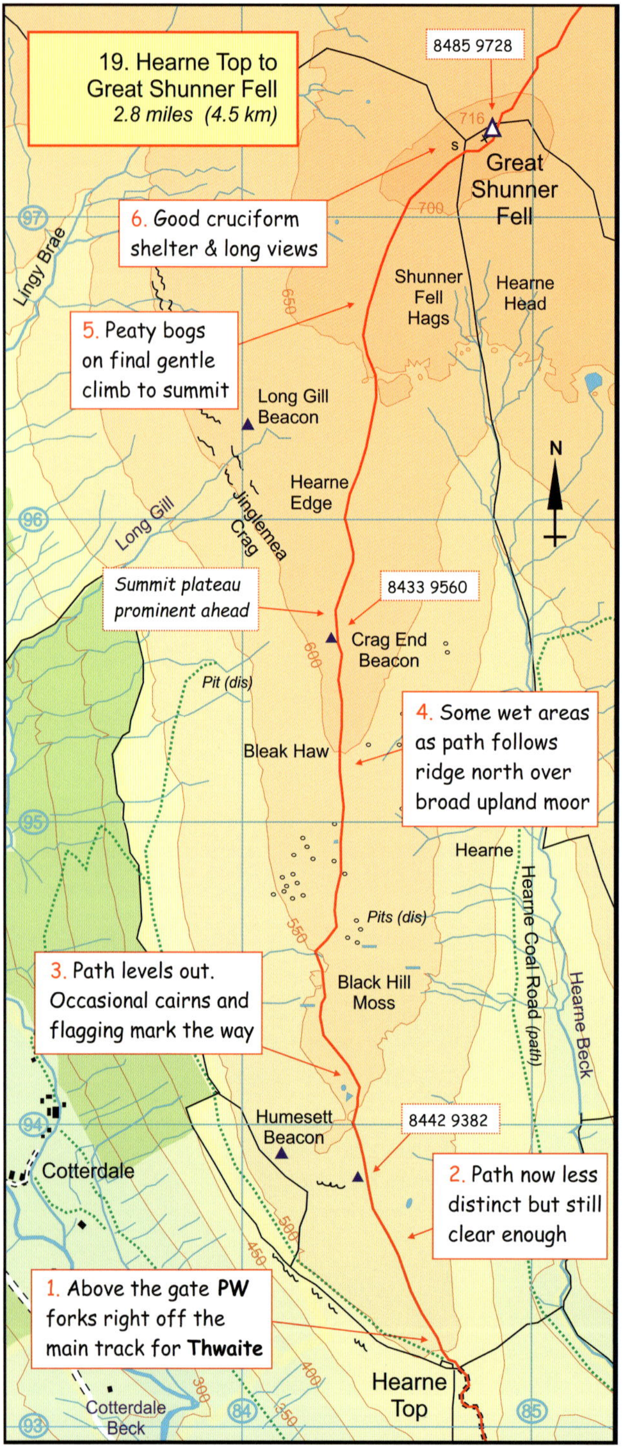

Beyond the next gate the way forks right with the long ridge ahead clearly curving right towards the summit.

Most of these broad Pennine fells are managed as grouse moors, and from early August onwards you may come across shooting parties, but if you stick to the path they shouldn't cause you any problems. The red grouse, which you will see and certainly hear cluck-clucking low across the heather, are the main target. The much rarer black grouse, now almost extinct in England, are being encouraged in the Dales and northern Pennines by schemes to improve their habitat, especially around the fringes of heather moors.

The upland moors support only a limited range of flora, mainly purple moor grass and heath rush, cotton grass and sphagnum mosses in the wetter areas, and of course heather and bracken. But they can be surprisingly colourful, giving a mosaic of greens, reds and browns, scattered white by the cotton grass in early summer and purple by the heather later in the year.

A cruciform shelter with a trig point built into one arm marks the summit, giving great views of the Lakeland fells to the west.

The descent is steeper, quick and straightforward. A stunning view of Swaledale opens up by a tall cairn, before the path crosses a wet, shallow saddle on slabs and drops again, curving east to join a rough track by a spoil heap. A walled lane leads to the final rocky descent where a right turn at the road soon leads you into the lovely village of Thwaite.

Swaledale opens out below

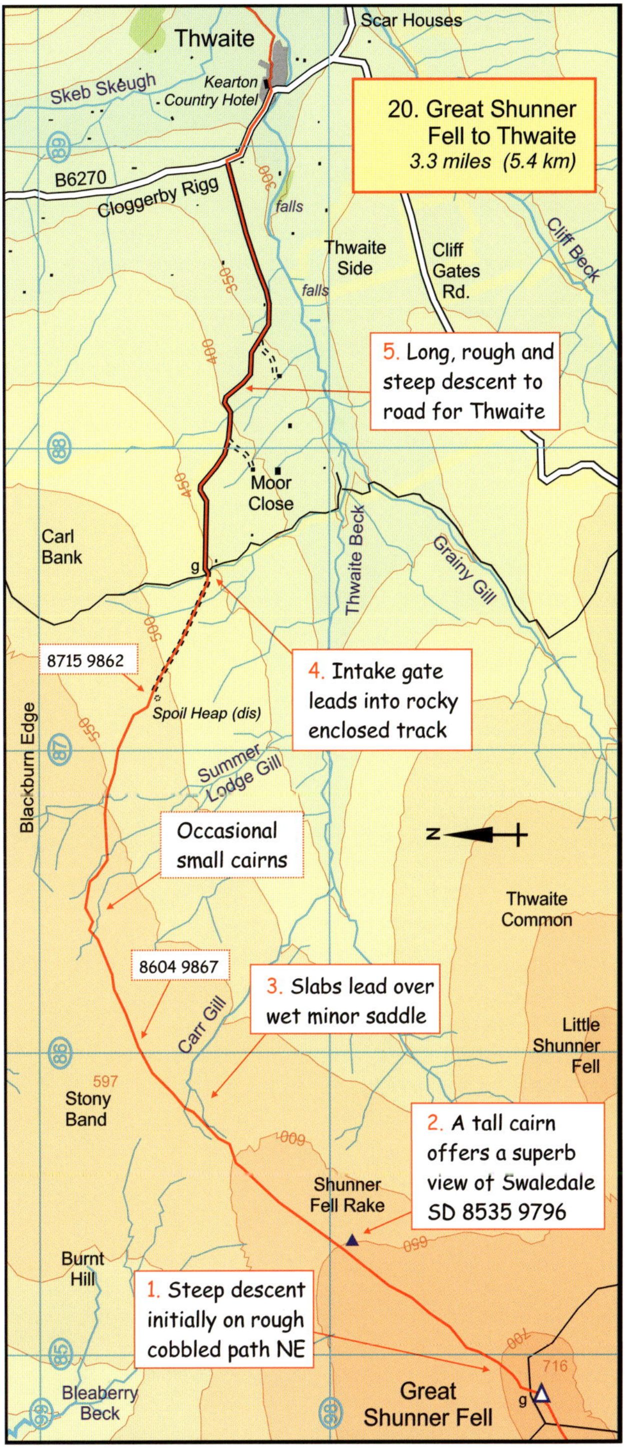

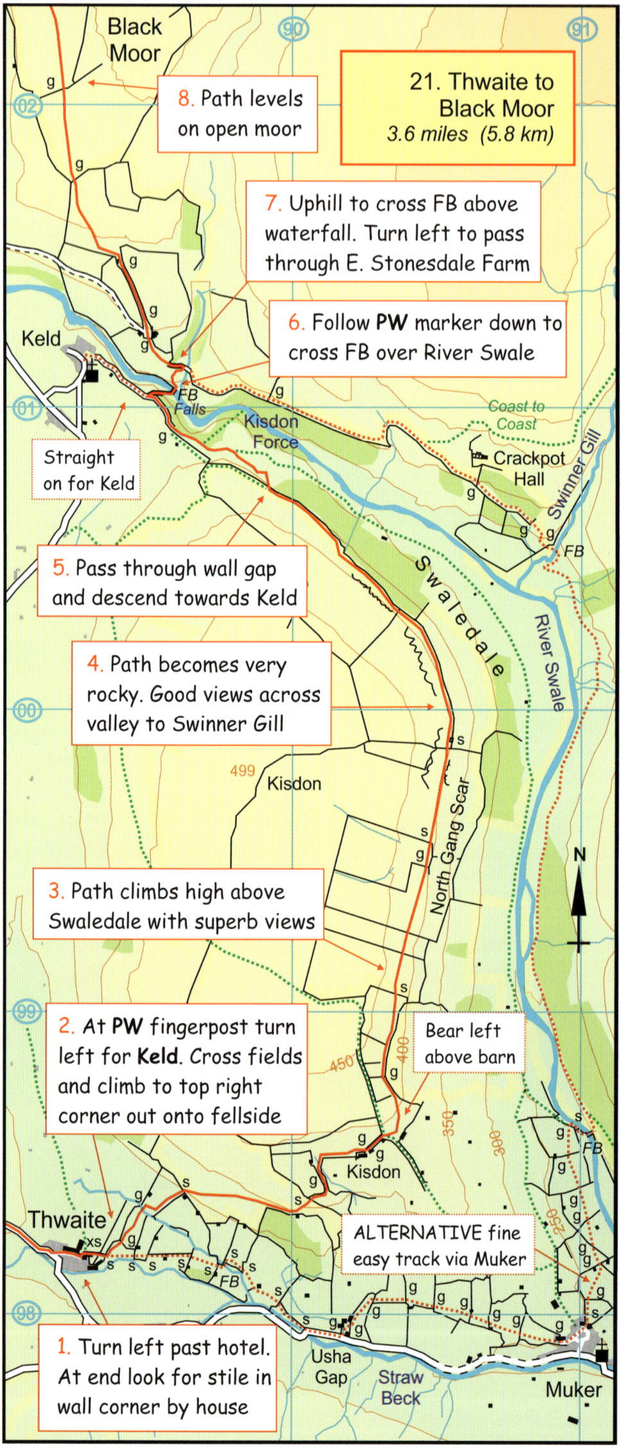

Thwaite

Head east through the village, passing the *Kearton Country Hotel*. A fingerpost for the **PW** to **Keld** points to a stile in the wall corner by a house, which leads into a narrow ginnel. At the second stile, adorned by an array of helpful signs, bear left across the field for **Keld** (or go straight ahead if the goal is Muker, one mile on).

The PW path heads NE, over a stream and uphill to a wall corner near a barn. A stile leads on to a rough path climbing east along the southern face of Kisdon Hill, with glorious views across the barn-strewn fields of Swaledale.

East Gill Force

Some care is needed here as the path twists and turns to finally pass Kisdon Farm. Bear left up an enclosed track and go straight on, curving left above another barn to head north, joining a wall on the right.

The path now levels, with the Swale far below on the right. Continue north, sticking to the contour to curve round the hill, with deep cut Swinner Gill prominent across the valley. Finally the path crosses a wall on the right to drop down towards **Keld**.

Cross the river at a footbridge and climb to another above East Gill Force Upper Falls. *Coast to Coast* walkers cross the bridge, but not you. Instead turn left for East Stonesdale Farm. Pass straight through, up along a walled track, bearing left above a barn to cross two fields and out onto Black Moor.

The path continues north, shadowing Stonesdale Beck down to the left and the road beyond it. In bad weather there are several opportunities to drop to the road if necessary.

Finally descend to cross Lad Gill at a clapper bridge. The path climbs steeply NE, turns north on a good track, then NE again at a fork.

Eventually a lone building comes into view - Britain's highest and most welcome pub at Tan Hill.

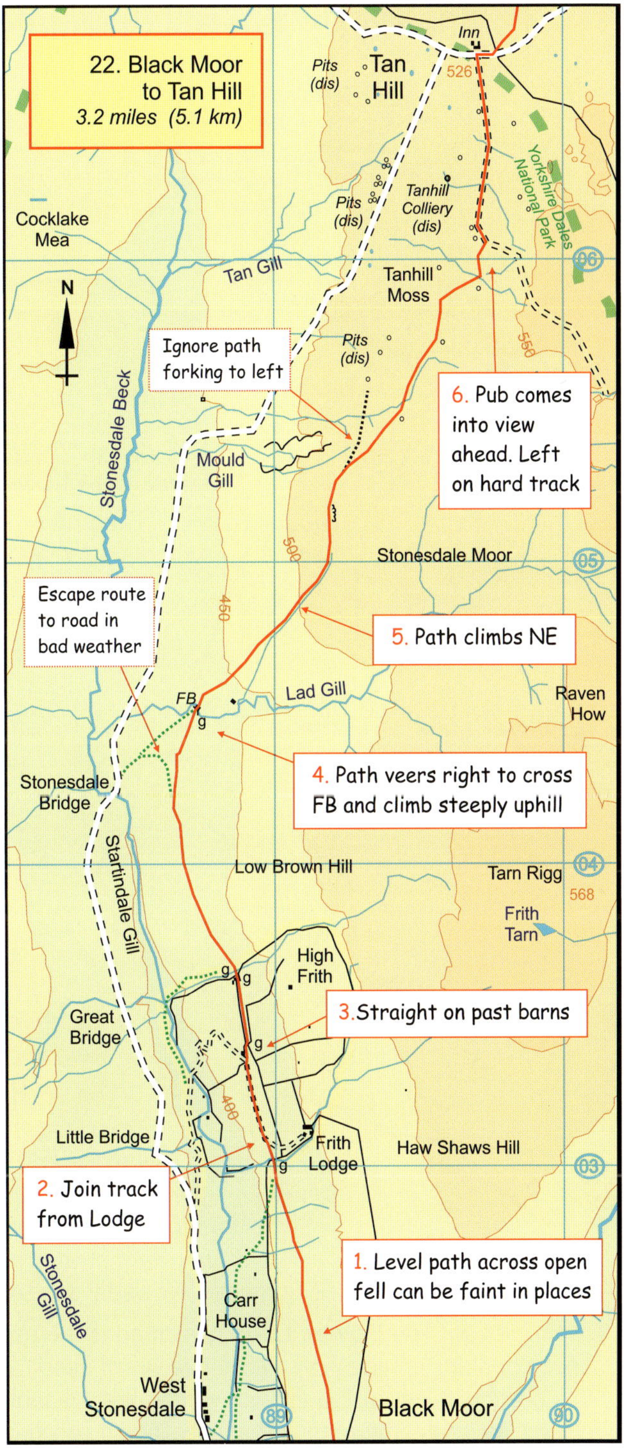

Section 6: **Tan Hill to Middleton-in-Teesdale**

16.6 miles (*26.7 km*)

Tan Hill Inn

The pub at Tan Hill dates from the 17th century and was created to serve the miners who worked the coal pits scattered across the moors nearby. Its exposed position brought it TV fame in a double glazing advert.

Tan Hill marks the spot where we say goodbye to the *Yorkshire Dales National Park*, and enter the *North Pennines Area of Outstanding Natural Beauty*, significant nationally for its extensive areas of blanket bog. Not surprisingly the going can be quite wet underfoot, particularly over Sleightholme Moor and Bowes Moor.

The Stainmore Gap, like the Aire Gap, is a significant pass through the Pennines and has been used since before the Bronze Age. The Romans built a road through it, linking forts at Bowes and Brough, as part of their strategy for taming the rebellious Brigantes. Nowadays the A66 follows the same route.

The **Bowes Loop**, which adds 3.6 miles overall, is an official and once popular Pennine Way alternative which used to offer the option of a break in this section. Alas, at the time of writing the Ancient Unicorn Inn at Bowes was closed, severely limiting the prospect of finding accommodation in the area.

The next 3 miles can be quite boggy after heavy rain, and difficult to navigate in mist - in either case you might prefer to stick to the road.

From the pub head east along the road. Just before a cattle grid the **PW** cuts off to the left for **Bowes**. The path sets off well enough, but soon descends to a boggy area where the track fades from view. A line of white topped posts mark the way, augmented by an occasional small cairn, but the route can be tricky at first as it heads NE. Ignore an array of small white pegs, which are concerned with grouse management and only serve to confuse matters.

The path curves gently ENE and picks up the line of Frumming Beck on the right. By the time you reach a tall concial cairn any navigational problems are behind you.

The route follows the beck, occasional lengths of duck board covering the worst of the wet areas. Eventually the path joins a hard track before crossing the beck at a metal bridge and up to join Sleightholme Moor Road.

Cairn at Frumming Beck

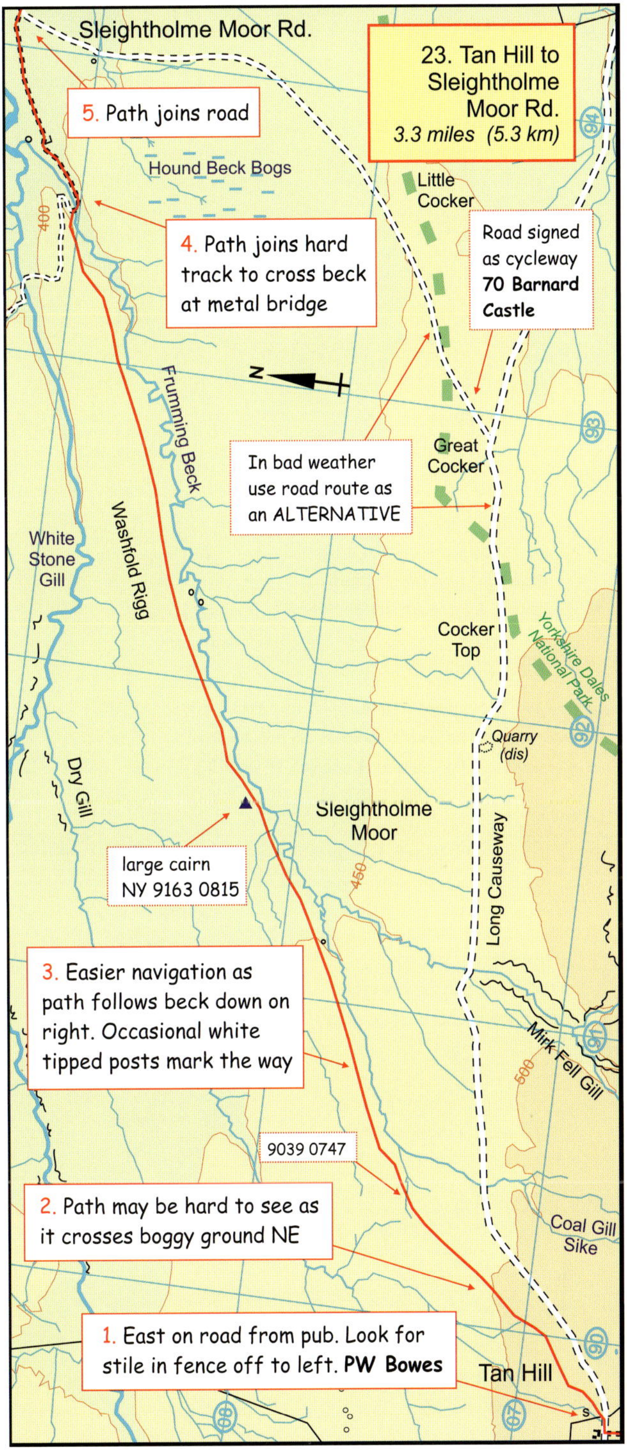

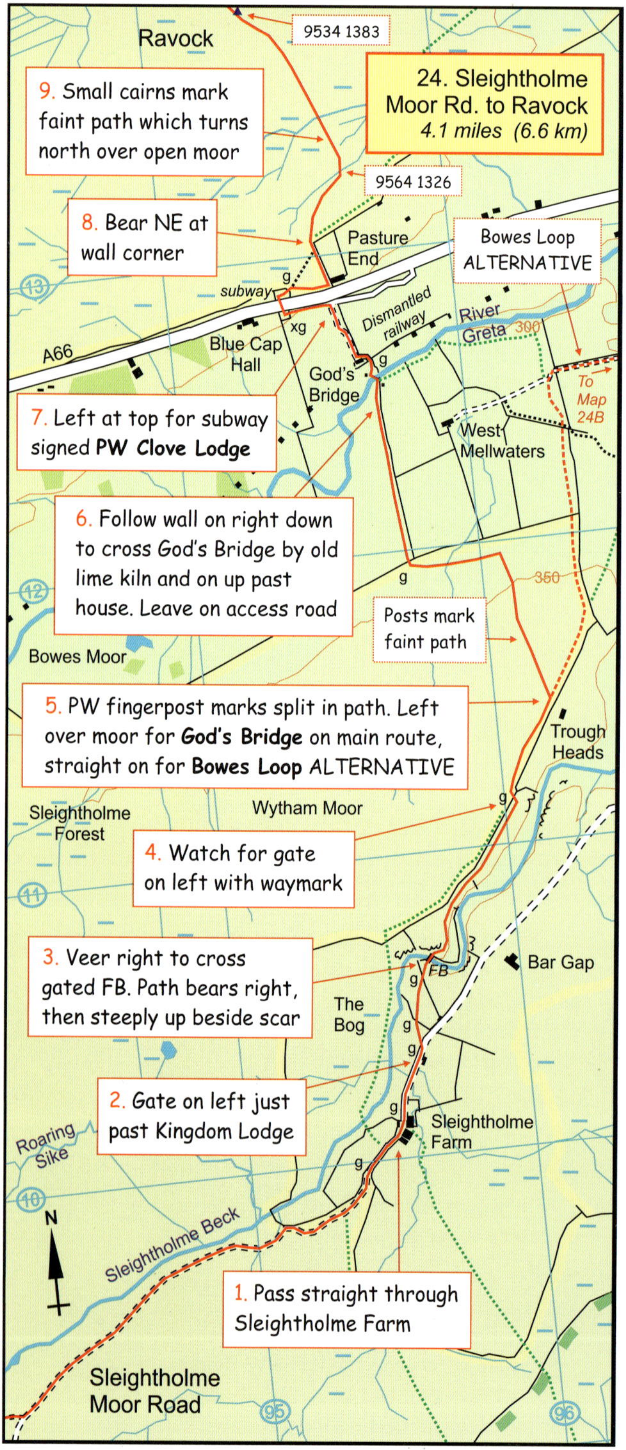

God's Bridge

The track passes through Sleightholme Farm, before the **PW** cuts left across fields to cross Sleightholme Beck. The path climbs to Trough Heads, where the route splits: straight on for the **Bowes Loop** or left across the edge of Wytham Moor for **God's Bridge**. The way drops to span the River Greta at this natural limestone crossing, before climbing between buttresses of the former Stainmore railway by a house and out along the access road. Bear left at the top to cross the busy A66 through an underpass, turning right on the far side and then left uphill by a wall for **Clove Lodge**.

The faint path curves right at the wall corner, the way marked by a post and small cairns, then at a stream bears NNW climbing onto the plateau of Ravock, site of a Bronze Age cairnfield.

Ravock, Bowes Moor

BOWES LOOP

*For **Bowes** keep straight on from Trough Heads following the wall on your right to join the road from West Mellwaters heading east. The path meanders as it follows the River Greta eastwards before crossing it just beyond Lady Myres. The path then cuts across several fields to pass around Bowes Castle and out onto the main road. The remains of the Norman keep stand at the corner of what was a Roman fort.*

Follow the road west, cross the A66 and go on to West Stoney Keld and Levy Pool to cross Deepdale Beck at a large footbridge (map 25). The way ahead is unclear, but head uphill northwards, dipping to cross Hazelgill Beck, then bear NE over wet ground to join a fence on the right, heading NNW.

Beyond a gate turn WNW, aiming for the left side of the prominent hill, Goldsborough. Again the path fades and the ground becomes very boggy, but look to cross Yawd Sike at a large metal bridge. The path skirts the southern flank of the hill before dropping to join tho road to Clove Lodge, rejoining the main route.

Bowes Castle

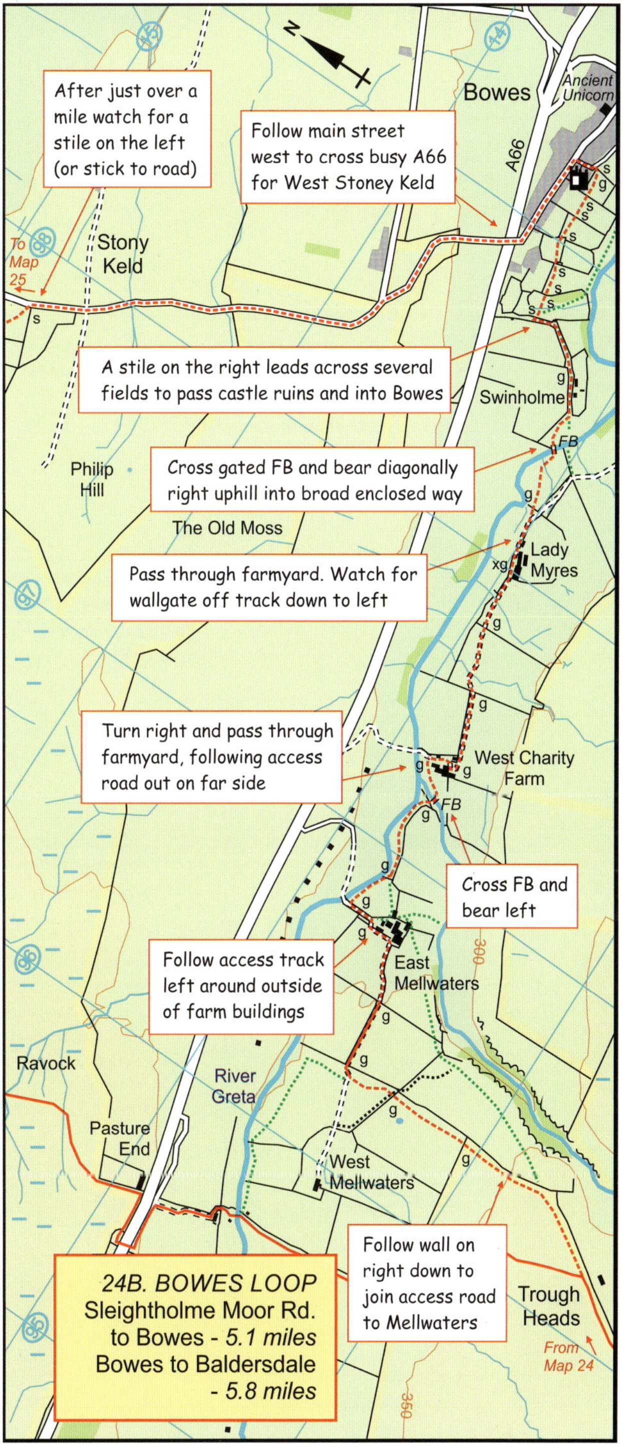

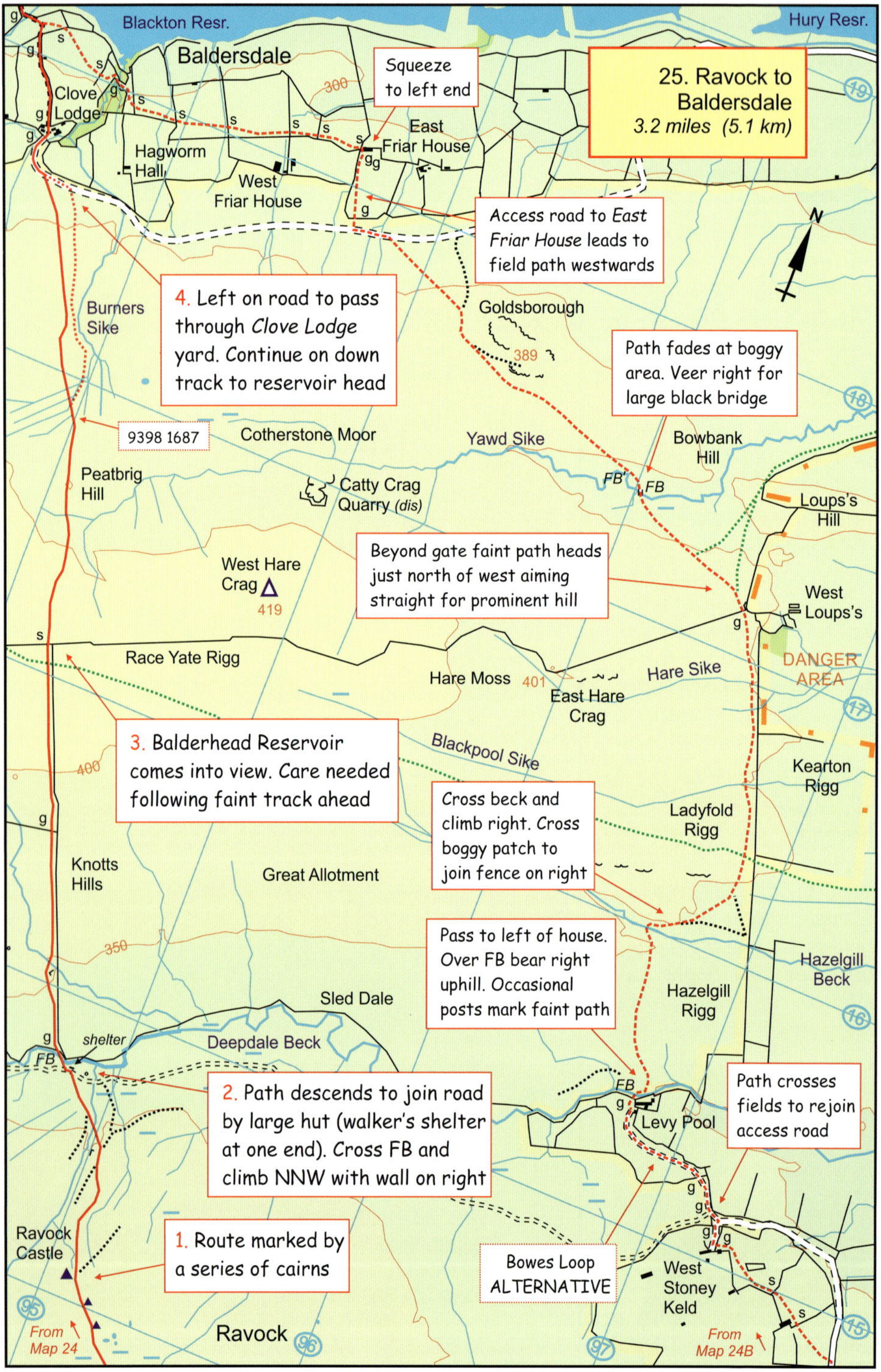
25. Ravock to Baldersdale
3.2 miles (5.1 km)
Blackton Resr.
Hury Resr.
Baldersdale
Clove Lodge
Hagworm Hall
West Friar House
East Friar House
Squeeze to left end
Access road to East Friar House leads to field path westwards
4. Left on road to pass through Clove Lodge yard. Continue on down track to reservoir head
Burners Sike
Goldsborough
389
Path fades at boggy area. Veer right for large black bridge
9398 1687
Cotherstone Moor
Yawd Sike
Bowbank Hill
Peatbrig Hill
Catty Crag Quarry (dis)
FB
Loups's Hill
Beyond gate faint path heads just north of west aiming straight for prominent hill
West Hare Crag
419
West Loups's
Race Yate Rigg
Hare Moss
401
East Hare Crag
Hare Sike
DANGER AREA
3. Balderhead Reservoir comes into view. Care needed following faint track ahead
Blackpool Sike
Kearton Rigg
Cross beck and climb right. Cross boggy patch to join fence on right
Ladyfold Rigg
Knotts Hills
Great Allotment
Pass to left of house. Over FB bear right uphill. Occasional posts mark faint path
Hazelgill Beck
Hazelgill Rigg
Sled Dale
shelter
Deepdale Beck
2. Path descends to join road by large hut (walker's shelter at one end). Cross FB and climb NNW with wall on right
Levy Pool
Path crosses fields to rejoin access road
Ravock Castle
1. Route marked by a series of cairns
Bowes Loop ALTERNATIVE
West Stoney Keld
Ravock
From Map 24
From Map 24B

The path drops to cross Deepdale Beck by a large hut, then continues NNW, a wall on the right leading the way to the cross fence at Race Yate Rigg. Balderhead Reservoir comes into view, as the faint path goes straight on across the open rough pasture of Cotherstone Moor, descending gently to join a road just before Clove Lodge. Pass through the Lodge yard and down to skirt the western end of Blackton Reservoir, turning north along the access road of Birk Hat farm.

The harsh life led by Hannah Hauxwell, who used to farm at Low Birk Hat without electricity or running water, was shown in a 1973 ITV documentary *Too Long a Winter* and she became a minor celebrity. Today her former rich meadows are designated a *Site of Special Scientific Interest*.

Another wall leads NNW across the moor past Kelton Hill, before descending north diagonally across meadows for Grassholme Reservoir in Lunedale.

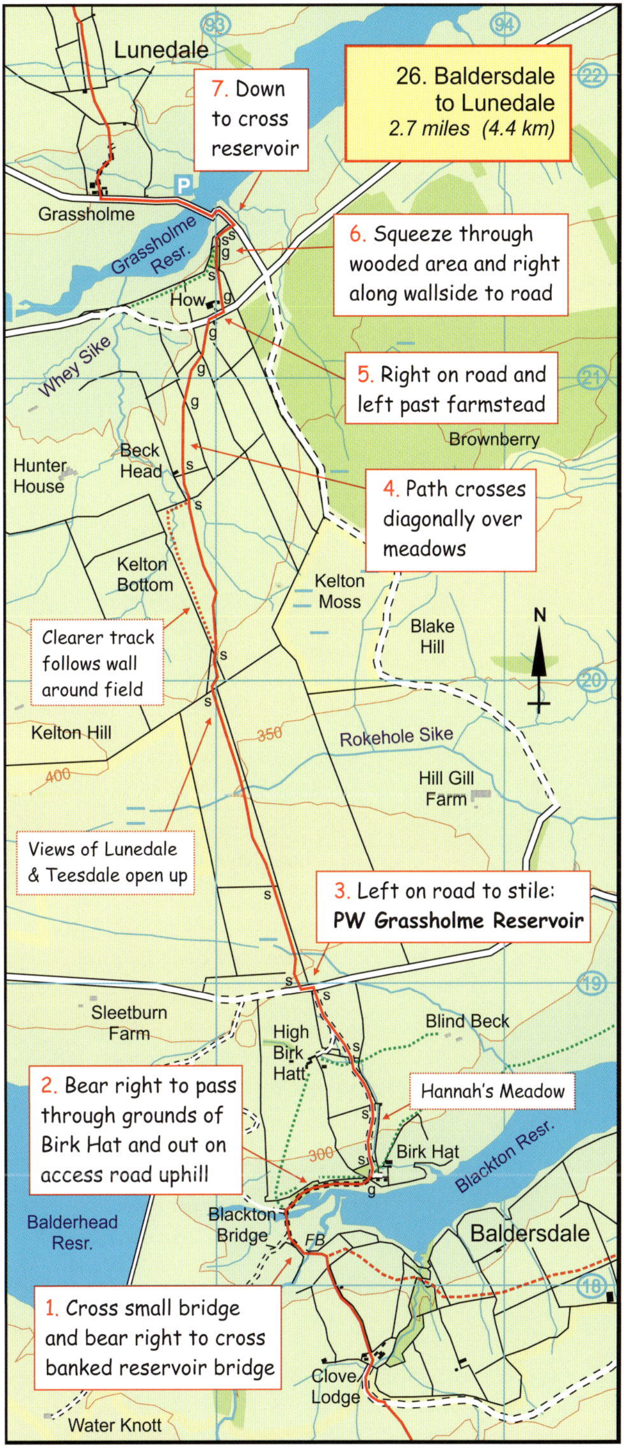

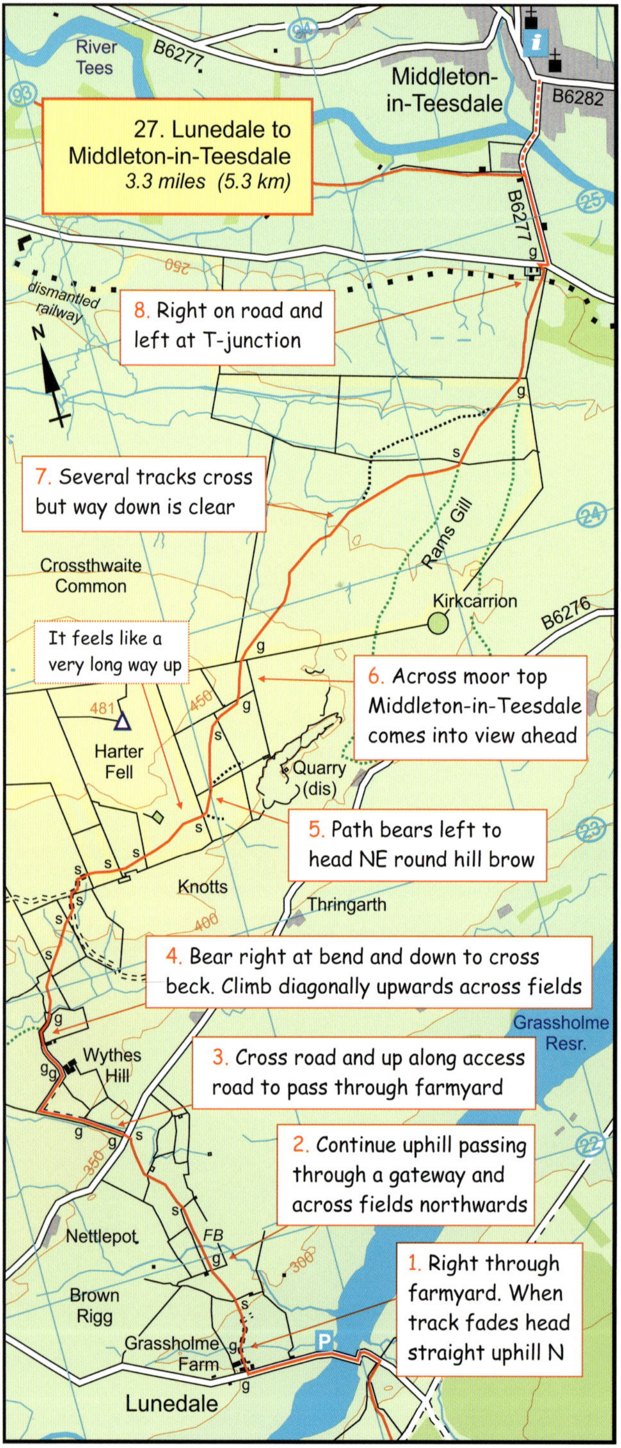

Follow the road across the reservoir and turn right through the yard of Grassholme Farm. The way curves right beyond, before turning straight up hill, across fields and out onto a road. Continue along the access road opposite to pass Wythes Hill Farm, following the track as it turns down to cross Carl Beck at a metal gate.

Some careful navigation is now required to follow the faint path diagonally uphill over several fields, bearing right to follow the contour and skirt the south eastern flank of Harter Fell, with fine views back across Lundale and Selset Reservoir.

After what seems an age the path finally climbs gently to cross the brow and Middleton-in-Teesdale comes enticingly into view ahead. All that remains is to head straight for it, NE downhill to join the B6277 across the River Tees and up into town.

This small market town grew significantly in the early 19th century when the *London Lead Company* – a Quaker lead mining enterprise – established its headquarters there. It's another useful spot for walkers, having everything you might need, including a tourist information centre, gift shops, bakers, tearooms, several good pubs and plenty of accommodation.

Lunedale (top); Middleton-in-Teesdale (above); Low Force, Teesdale (below); Driving sheep above High Cup Nick (right)

Section 7: **Middleton-in-Teesdale to Dufton**

20.2 miles (*32.5 km*)

This section is undoubtedly one of the most exciting and memorable of the whole walk.

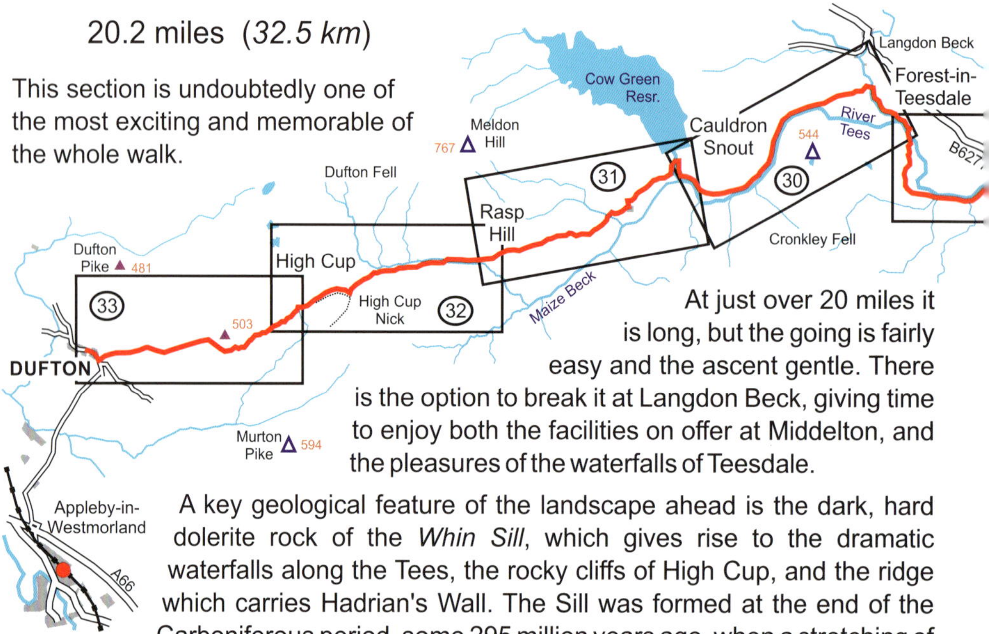

At just over 20 miles it is long, but the going is fairly easy and the ascent gentle. There is the option to break it at Langdon Beck, giving time to enjoy both the facilities on offer at Middelton, and the pleasures of the waterfalls of Teesdale.

A key geological feature of the landscape ahead is the dark, hard dolerite rock of the *Whin Sill*, which gives rise to the dramatic waterfalls along the Tees, the rocky cliffs of High Cup, and the ridge which carries Hadrian's Wall. The Sill was formed at the end of the Carboniferous period, some 295 million years ago, when a stretching of the earth's crust allowed a surge of molten rock at over 1,000 °C to rise from deep in the earth, diverting horizontally before reaching the surface, injecting itself between layers of limestone, shale and sandstone. The rock cooled to form a solid layer 70 metres thick under much of north east England. Erosion has brought it to the surface.

Following an easy riverside stroll, the route heads west to cross one of the loneliest, wildest stretches of open moorland on the entire route. The spectacular glacial chasm of High Cup is the finale, before a gentle descent into the Eden Valley to Dufton. Appleby, three miles to the south, provides a useful staging post on the walk.

River Tees and Cronkley Fell

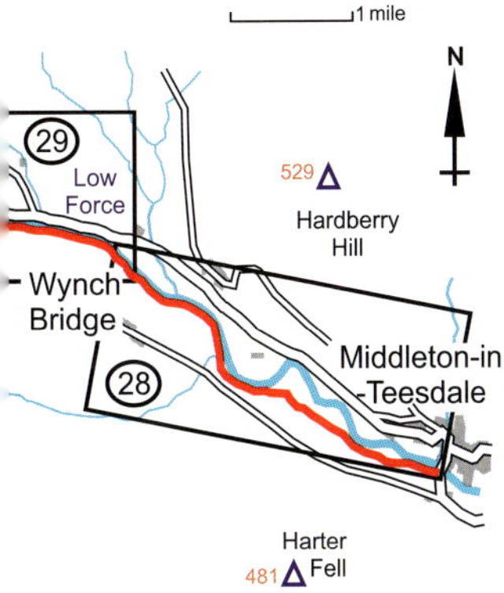

From the town rejoin the **PW** by heading south to cross the River Tees and turn right along a track just past the cattle market. The track follows the river NW, keeping straight on when the river loops away.

The path closes on the river again near Park End Woods, climbing high above it before dropping down to cross Rowten Beck at a footbridge. A couple of stiles lead back to the riverside, which is followed closely now.

Pass the wooden *Scoberry Bridge* on the right and soon enter the *Moor House – Upper Teesdale National Nature Reserve*, one of the largest in England covering 88 square kilometres of special upland habitats. The reserve is famous for its unique Arctic-Alpine plants which have survived here since the last Ice Age, conserved by traditional farming and moorland management practices.

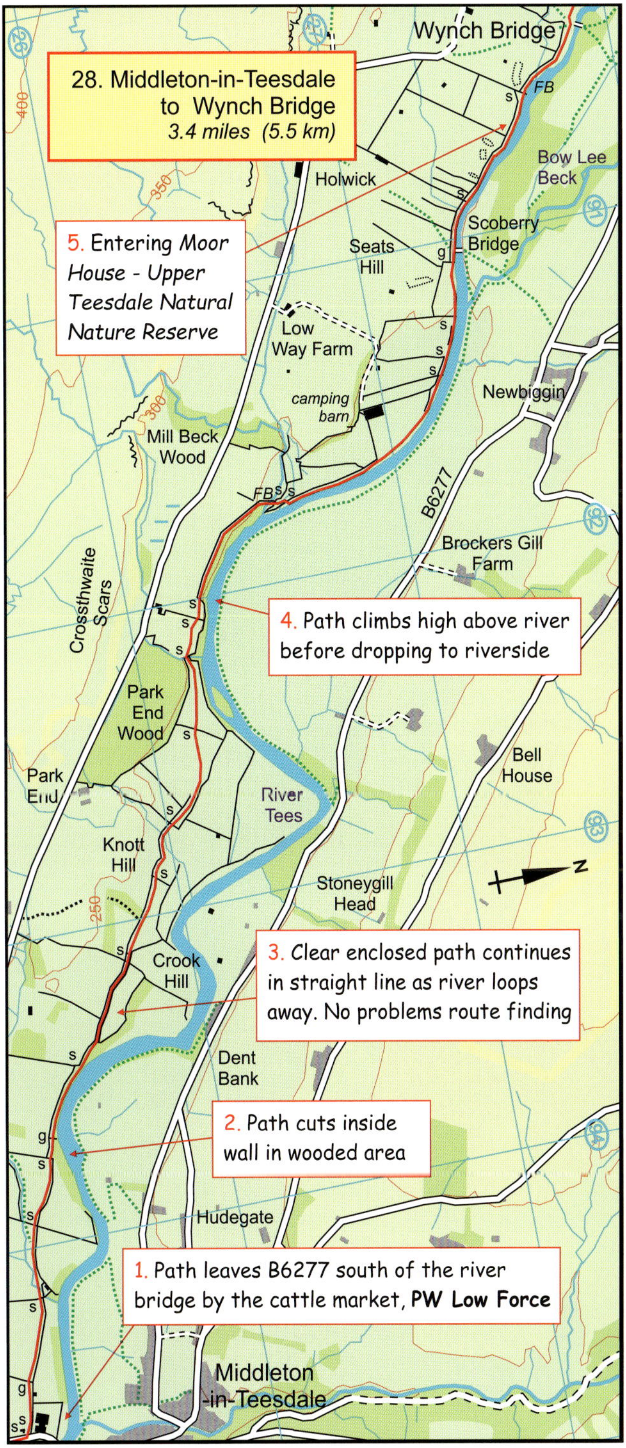

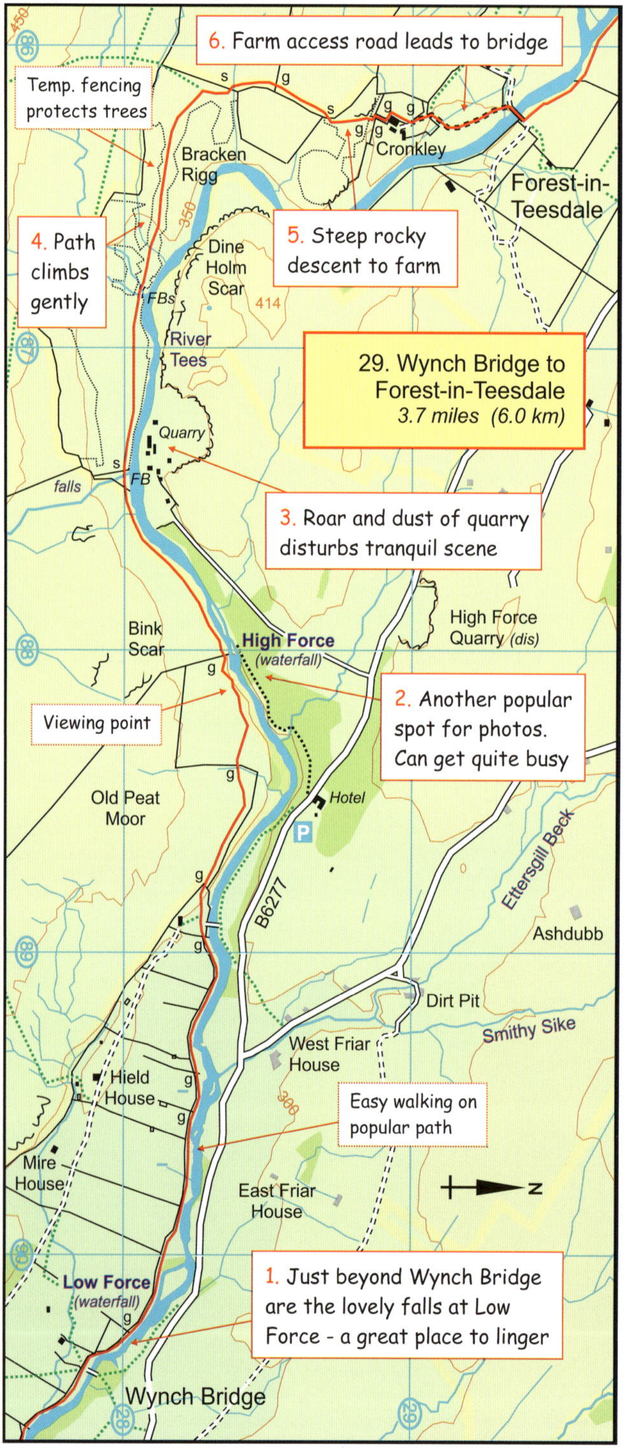

High Force, Teesdale

Wynch Bridge, Britain's oldest suspension bridge, is reached soon afterwards, giving superb views of Low Force waterfalls ahead. Originally built by miners in 1740, the current bridge dates from 1830. The previous bridge collapsed in 1802 when three men were crossing. One drowned.

The way continues on a popular stretch of track, past Holwick Head Bridge and on to High Force, not perhaps the biggest but certainly the most spectacular waterfall in England, as it cascades through a gap in the Whin Sill to drop 21 metres.

Beyond the waterfall, the increasing solitude is fractured by the sound of quarrying across the river, before the path climbs to curve north across Bracken Rigg and down through Cronkley Farm to cross the River Tees at Cronkley Bridge.

The **Pennine Way** now follows the north east bank of the Tees, past the confluence with Harwood Beck, to reach Saur Hill Bridge across the beck. The hostel is up a road to the right. Cross the bridge, heading for **Cauldron Snout**. The hotel at Langdon Beck can be reached by following the beck north to Intake Farm and crossing the road bridge there. Otherwise, follow the access road up to the farm at Sayer Hill, bearing left before it.

A faint path now crosses open pasture heading WSW to rejoin the River Tees by Widdy Bank Farm. The path ahead is clear, but eventually narrows and negotiating the rocky path is tricky. The path eases as it curves west beneath the Whin Sill outcrop at Falcon Clints, leading to an exciting scramble beside the gushing waters of Cauldron Snout.

Cauldron Snout

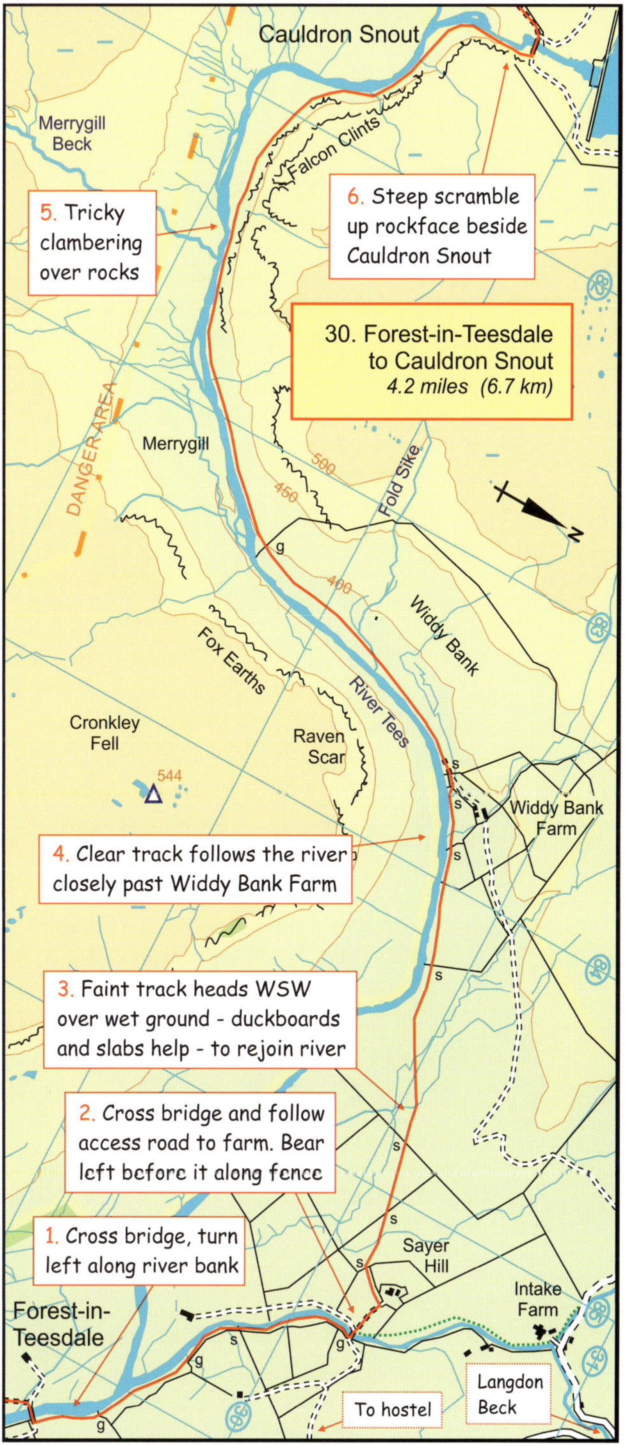

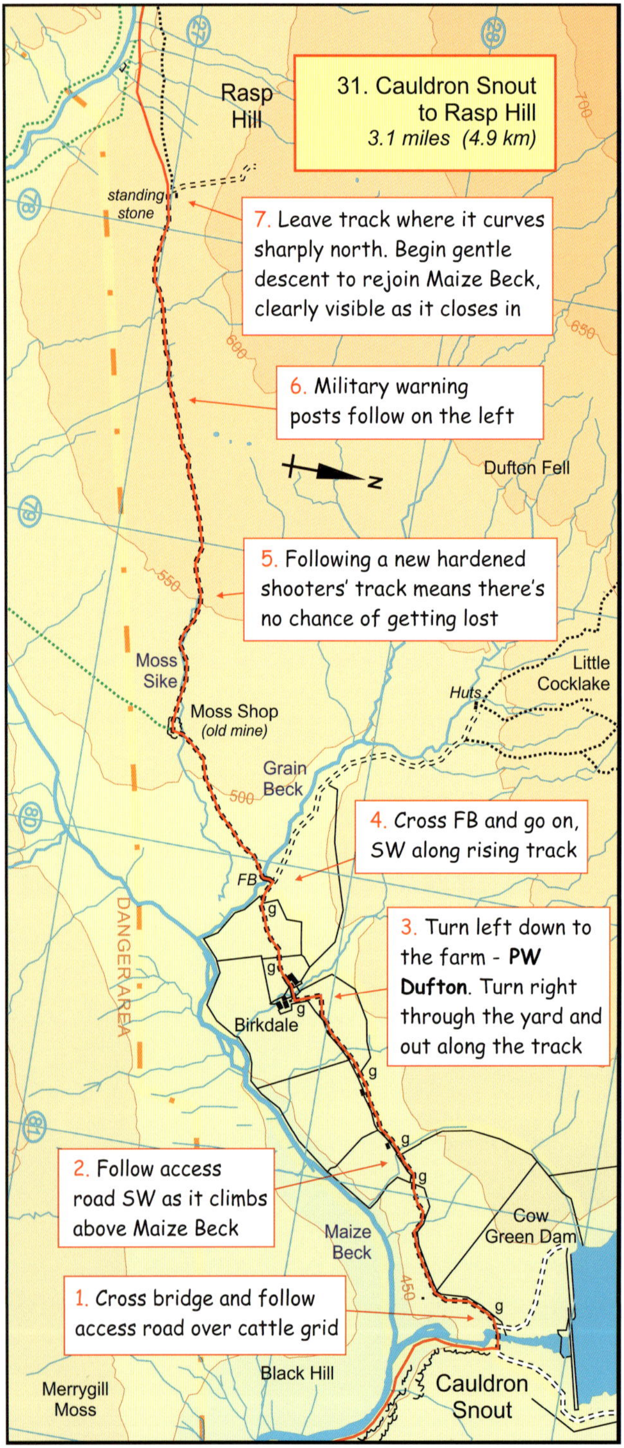

The Tees is crossed on a road bridge at the top of Cauldron Snout, beneath the dam walls of Cow Green Reservoir, constructed in 1971. Follow the access road to pass through Birkdale Farm.

This remote farm is said to be the highest occupied farmstead in England. It featured in ITV's 1973 documentary *Too Long a Winter* and was the setting for an historic 1948 photograph of a group of pioneering Pennine Way politicians led by Tom Stephenson.

The path continues SW with Maize Beck below to the left. After crossing Grain Beck the path climbs to an old lead mine on a newly hardened shooters' track alongside Moss Sike. The stony track continues all the way to Rasp Hill, shadowed by a line of military warning posts to the left, before leaving it at a right bend.

Tom Stephenson described this part as *the wildest and loneliest crossing in the whole of the Pennines*. Eventually the path descends to rejoin Maize Beck beneath Rasp Hill.

Maize Beck

The path follows the north bank of the beck, heading west, before crossing to the other side at a prominent metal footbridge. A good path continues westwards, climbing above the beck and out onto High Cup Plain where the beck curves away north.

The path forks to the right, and suddenly the awesome chasm of High Cup appears. The path leads down to the *Nick* – a gap at the *V* of the valley head where a thin stream trickles down between the vertical buttresses of the Whin Sill. This is a spot to stop and savour. The path itself continues along the northern rim of the valley.

Approaching High Cup

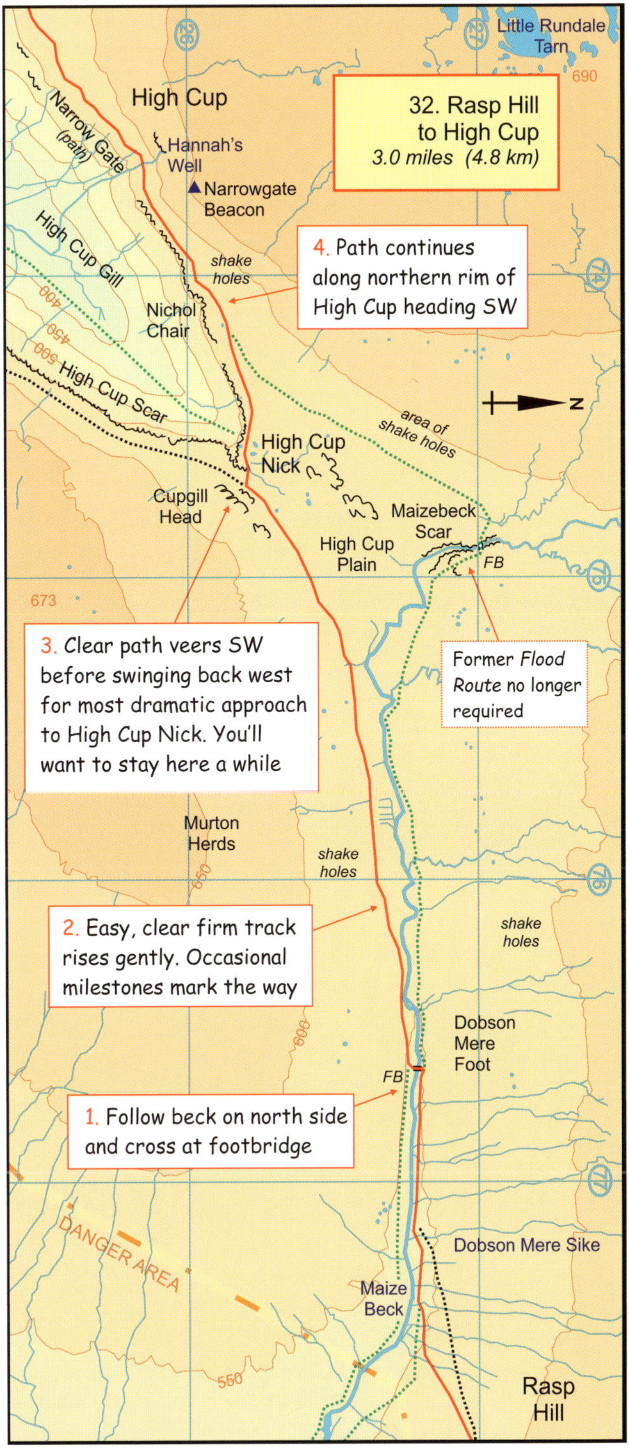

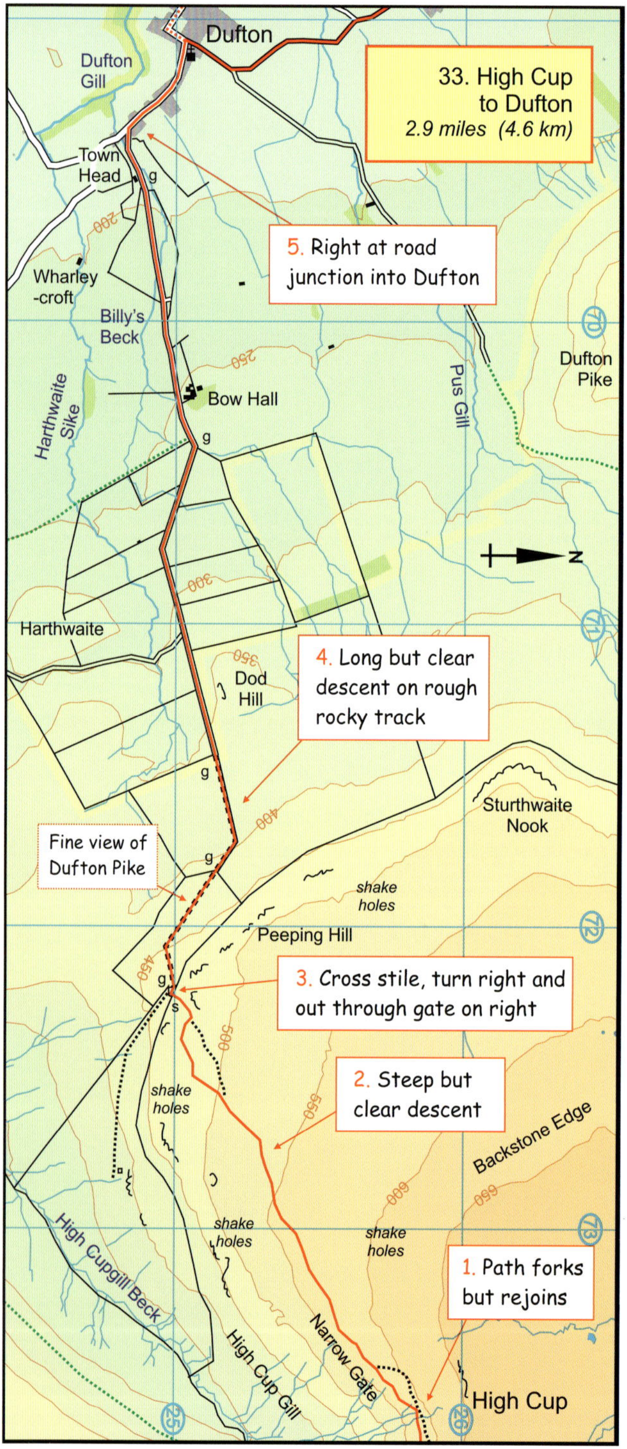

There is no difficulty finding your way down from High Cup. The track, called *Narrow Gate*, follows the rim SW to begin a fairly steep but clear descent. Beyond a sheep fold it picks up a stony track bearing northwest with the conical mound of Dufton Pike prominent ahead. The path soon becomes an enclosed track turning west, then eventually right at a T-junction along a road leading into Dufton. The **Pennine Way** cuts off right by a church, but you will want to follow the road left into the heart of the village.

Dufton, with its bright red sandstone houses, is a typical Westmorland village, complete with welcoming pub and handy youth hostel.

The bustling town of Appleby-in-Westmorland, on the Settle-Carlisle railway line, lies just 3 miles to the south, and can be reached by walking or by taxi, making it a perfect staging post for breaking the walk.

Dufton

High Cup Nick

Knock Old Man, with Great Dun Fell and Cross Fell beyond (above left); Greg's Hut (above right); Shelter and trig point on Cross Fell summit (below).

Section 8: **Dufton to Alston**

19.3 miles (*31.1 km*)

This section is without doubt the toughest of the whole walk. In good, clear weather there is little problem route finding, but you are much more likely to encounter misty and wet conditions and great care must be taken navigating across the featureless fell tops. Confidence using a compass bearing or GPS is essential.

Sometimes a fast prevailing north-easterly wind flows across the broad upland range of the north Pennines before plunging rapidly over the western edge. This is the Helm Wind. It is often characterised by a band of cloud along the ridge shrouding the fell tops in mist.

Cross Fell is the highest point on the route and the highest point in England outside Lakeland. It is a vast, flat rocky plateau with a cruciform shelter and trig point towards the western rim. Once beyond Cross Fell there are no more navigation difficulties.

The fells here are scarred by the remnants of lead mining. Hushes – great gouges in the hillside – are the result of a particular mining technique where dammed water was suddenly released to scour away the surface soil and reveal ore veins. Mine shafts abound, so care is needed to avoid wandering too far from the path.

The Pennine Way officially leaves Dufton on a track by the church at the east end of the village heading for **Garrigill**, to follow a rough track curving behind the village. But it is easier from the village green to follow the road northwest and at the west end of the village pick up an enclosed footpath to rejoin the Pennine Way.

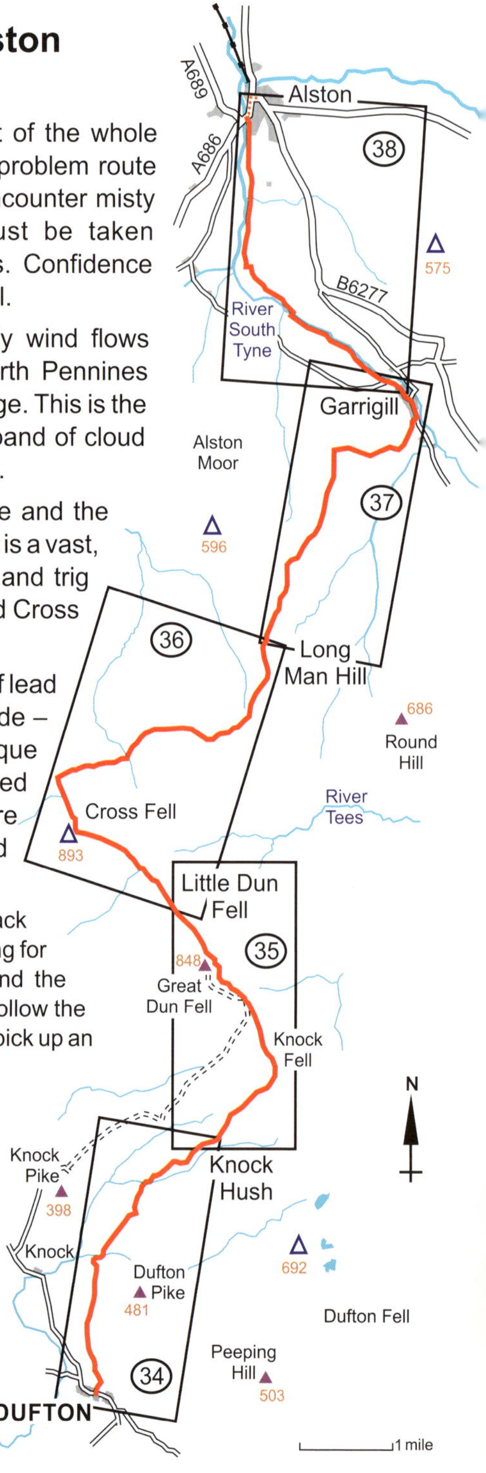

Knock Pike with Lakeland beyond

The track leads through Coatsike Farm and into a tree-lined track – *Hurning Lane* - which continues north to pass the ruined farmstead of Halsteads.

The track curves and drops to cross Great Rundale Beck on a stone clapper bridge, then climbs NE.

You are now passing between the distinctive conical hills of Dufton Pike (*right*) and Knock Pike (*left*). The *Pikes* are made of ancient Silurian slates and volcanic rocks which predate the Carboniferous rocks of the Pennines.

Beyond a second gate the track eventually turns left uphill and the **PW** leaves the track by a fingerpost, curving round the hillside to cross the rock-strewn Swindale Beck on a large metal footbridge, entering another part of the *Moor House – Upper Teesdale National Nature Reserve*.

The way lies steeply uphill NE. Two gatepost cairns show the way, leading on up to a larger cairn amidst a rocky clearing. One of a series of small marker stones points the way up alongside Knock Hush.

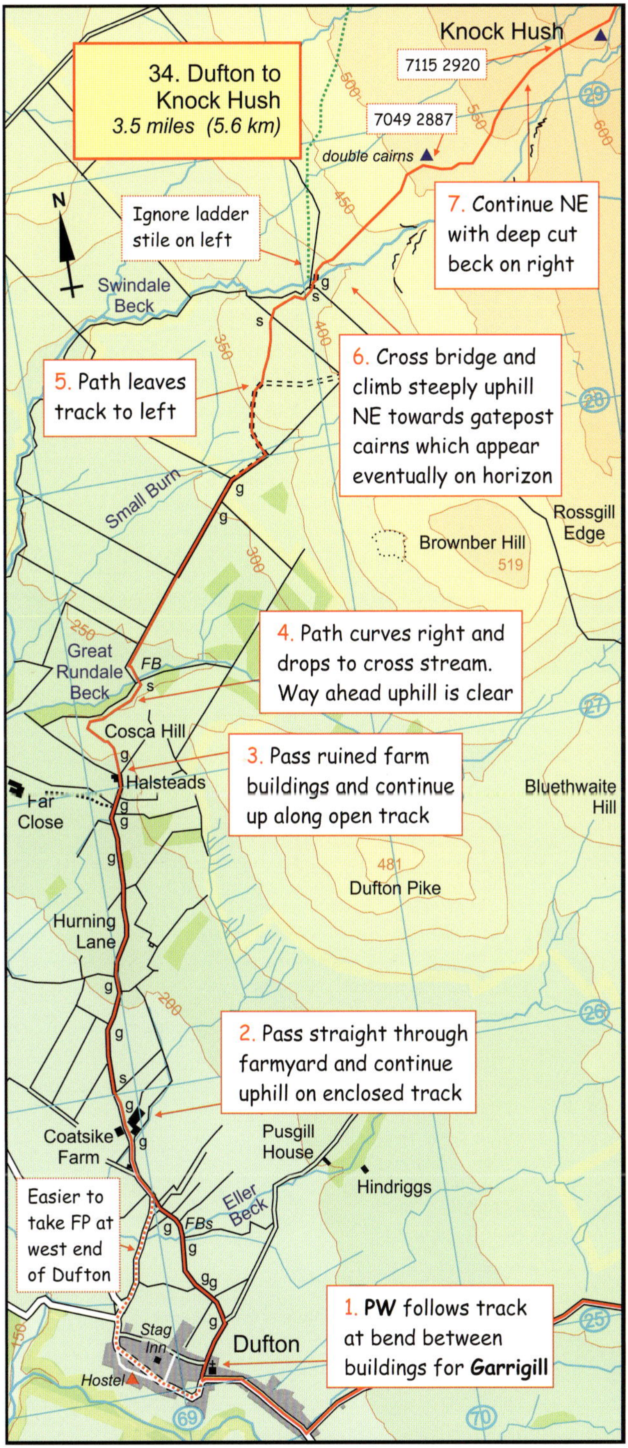

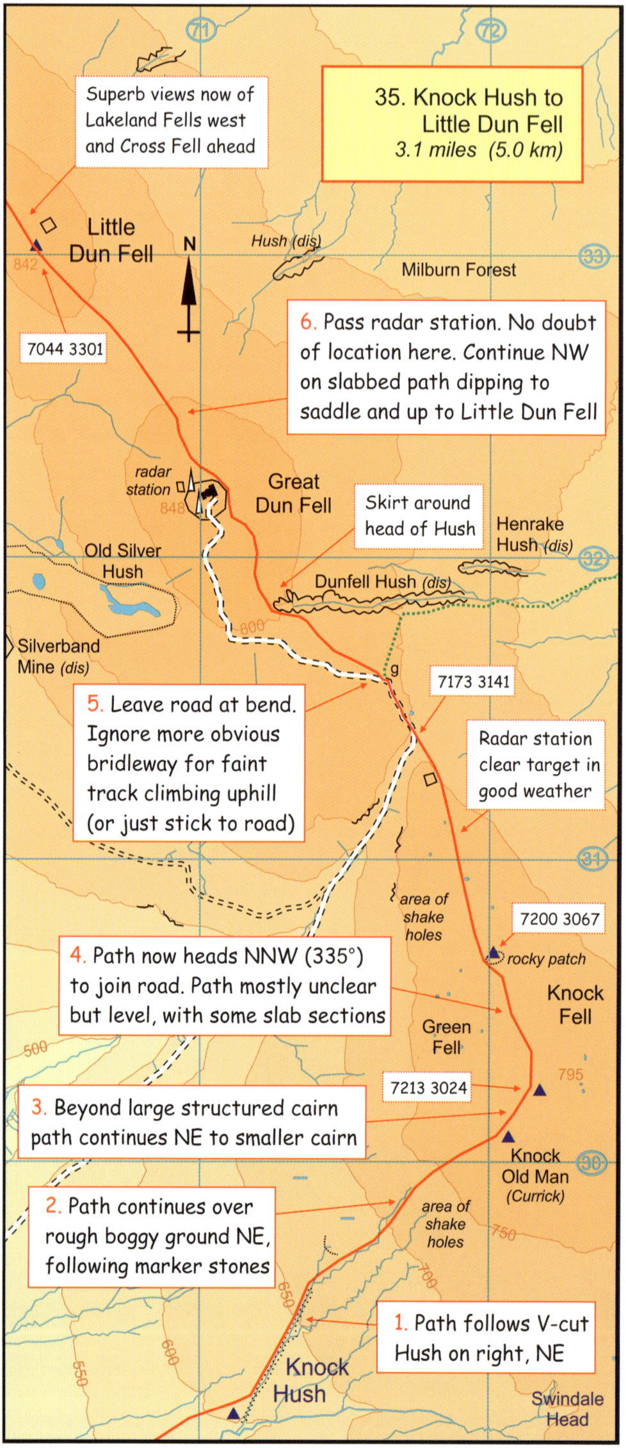

The faint grassy track winds NE over boggy ground to the tall structured cairn of Knock Old Man. Go straight on to another smaller cairn, before turning NNW. In clear weather the target is the radar station; in mist the faint track soon disappears and care is needed using compass or GPS. The way ahead is essentially level, dropping gently. It is better to err slightly to the left, the aim being to join the tarmac road up to the station.The **PW** cuts off to the right, bearing NW to skirt the top of Dunfell Hush and pass to the right of the radar station.

The path continues NW, dipping to a saddle, but stone slabbing leads all the way to Little Dun Fell.

Continue NW, across another saddle with occasional stone slabs, to ascend the rocky bank to Cross Fell. Once on the plateau locate a tall cairn, which leads the way WNW to another, then on to the trig point and shelter. If you get lost in mist here, head west to locate the rim of the plateau, which you can then follow, right, clockwise.

From the shelter a series of small cairns mark the way, just west of north, to the rim and down to join the Corpse Road. You are now safe. The road leads east, past Greg's Hut – a bothy that offers useful respite from bad weather. The long clear track follows Backstone Edge before curving north.

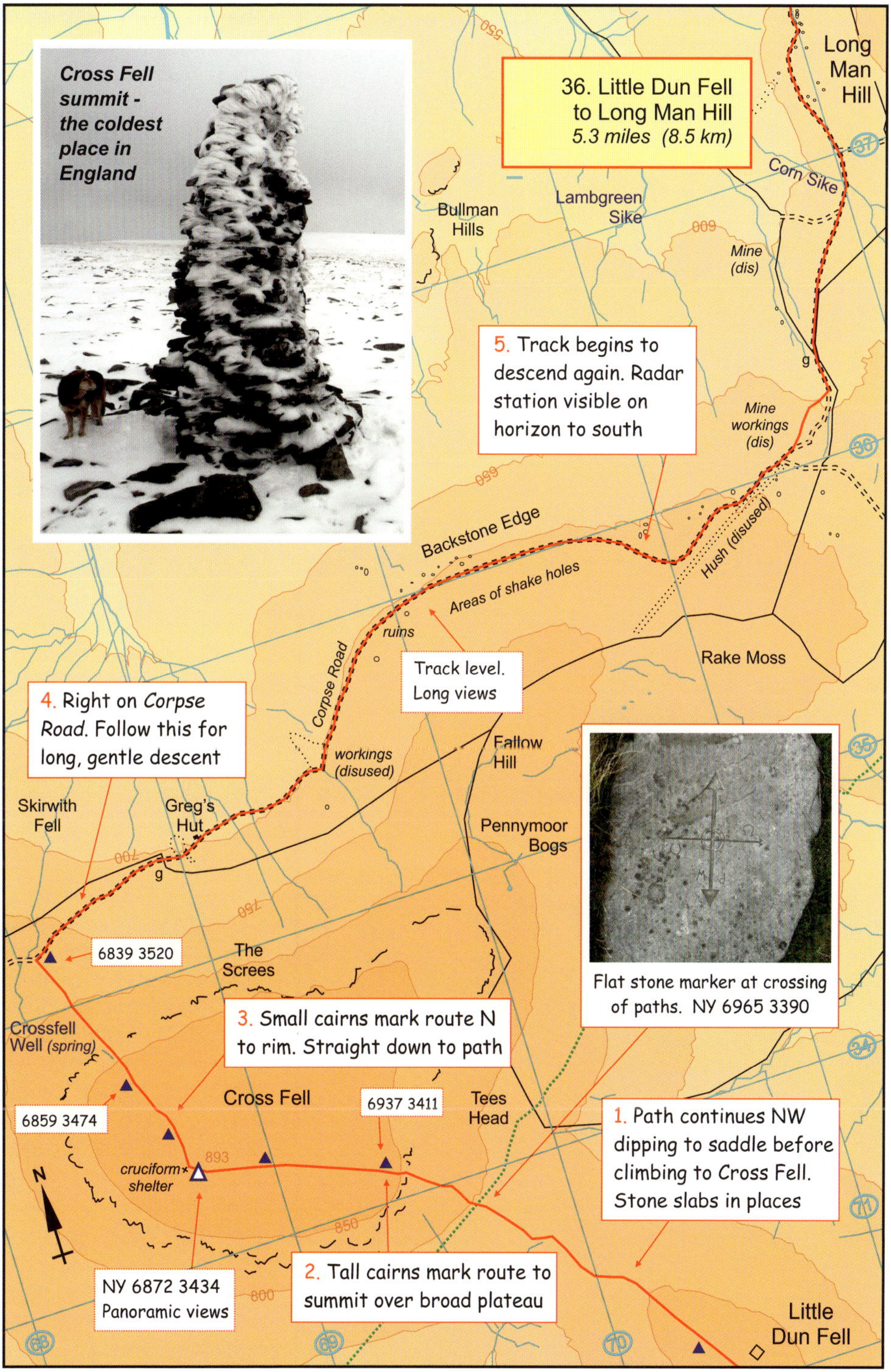
36. Little Dun Fell to Long Man Hill
5.3 miles (8.5 km)
Cross Fell summit - the coldest place in England
Long Man Hill
Corn Sike
Lambgreen Sike
Bullman Hills
Mine (dis)
5. Track begins to descend again. Radar station visible on horizon to south
Mine workings (dis)
Backstone Edge
Hush (disused)
Areas of shake holes
ruins
Corpse Road
Track level. Long views
Rake Moss
4. Right on Corpse Road. Follow this for long, gentle descent
workings (disused)
Fallow Hill
Skirwith Fell
Greg's Hut
Pennymoor Bogs
6839 3520
The Screes
Flat stone marker at crossing of paths. NY 6965 3390
Crossfell Well (spring)
3. Small cairns mark route N to rim. Straight down to path
Cross Fell
6859 3474
6937 3411
Tees Head
1. Path continues NW dipping to saddle before climbing to Cross Fell. Stone slabs in places
cruciform shelter
893
850
800
NY 6872 3434
Panoramic views
2. Tall cairns mark route to summit over broad plateau
Little Dun Fell
N
550
600
650
700
750
37
36
35
34
71
68
69
70

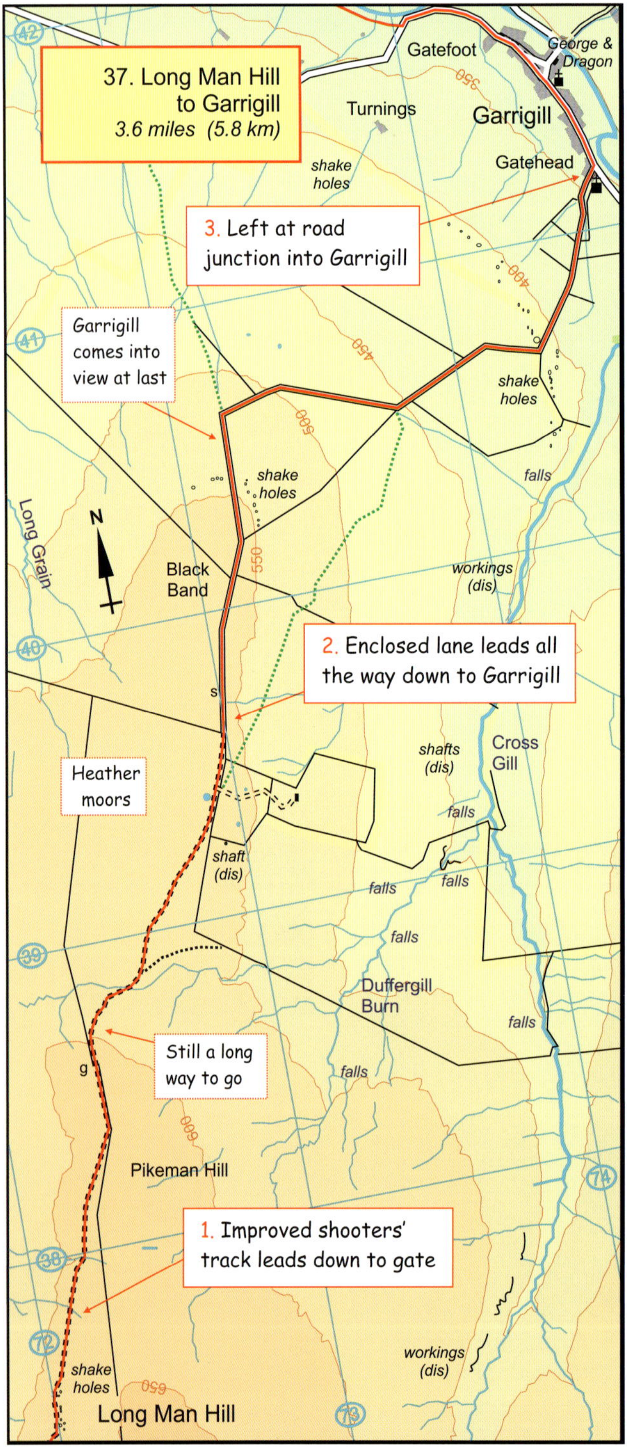

The long, hard track down to Garrigill descends slowly NNE. Eventually the lane turns east to drop more steeply to the tiny village, which is now clearly in view.

If accommodation can be found, this is the first opportunity to break the day, otherwise it's another four miles alongside the River South Tyne to Alston.

Follow the main street north through Garrigill. Where it curves west by the river, take a gate on the right, for both the **PW** and **South Tyne Trail** for **Alston**.

It would be hard to get completely lost here as the path follows the river all the way, but there are tedious twists and bends through fields where you can easily take a wrong turn, so pay close attention to the map.

The path climbs above the river before closing in again, and may become overgrown. Cross the river at a large metal footbridge.

Beyond a wall gap the path keeps right along the edge of a widening field, climbing the bank to pass Low Sillyhall. The path goes on NW across fields, to cut left through Bleagate Farm, then onwards, curving north now. Eventually, high above the river you pass a cemetery, then the hostel, and you're in Alston.

The **Pennine Way** cuts down left to cross the river; go straight on for England's highest market town.

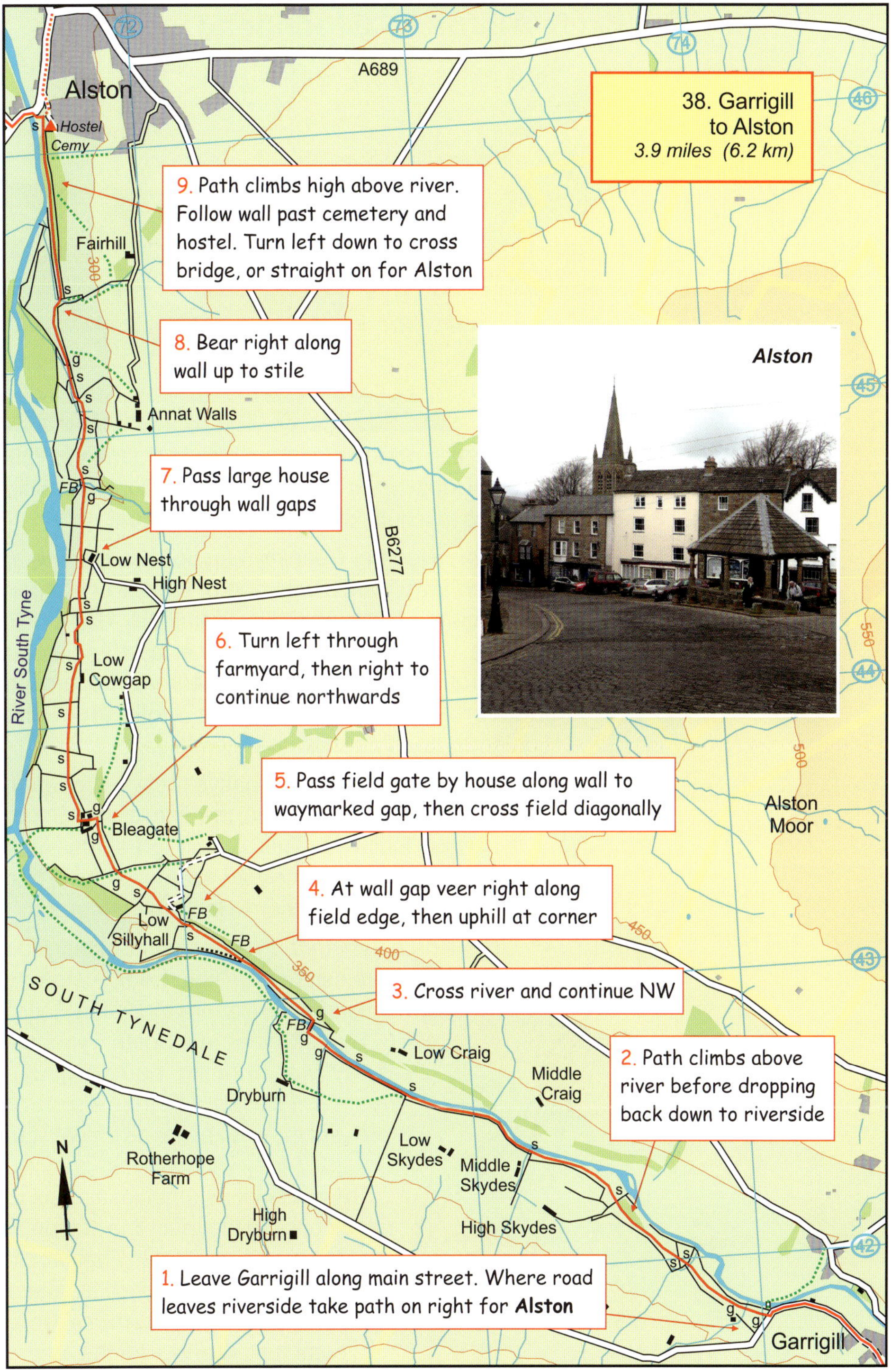
38. Garrigill
to Alston
3.9 miles (6.2 km)
1. Leave Garrigill along main street. Where road leaves riverside take path on right for **Alston**
2. Path climbs above river before dropping back down to riverside
3. Cross river and continue NW
4. At wall gap veer right along field edge, then uphill at corner
5. Pass field gate by house along wall to waymarked gap, then cross field diagonally
6. Turn left through farmyard, then right to continue northwards
7. Pass large house through wall gaps
8. Bear right along wall up to stile
9. Path climbs high above river. Follow wall past cemetery and hostel. Turn left down to cross bridge, or straight on for Alston
Alston
Alston
Hostel
Cemy
A689
B6277
Fairhill
Annat Walls
Low Nest
High Nest
Low
Cowgap
Bleagate
Low
Sillyhall
River South Tyne
SOUTH TYNEDALE
Low Craig
Middle
Craig
Dryburn
Low
Skydes
Middle
Skydes
High Skydes
Rotherhope
Farm
High
Dryburn
Alston
Moor
Garrigill
N

Section 9: **Alston to Greenhead**

16.6 miles (*26.7 km*)

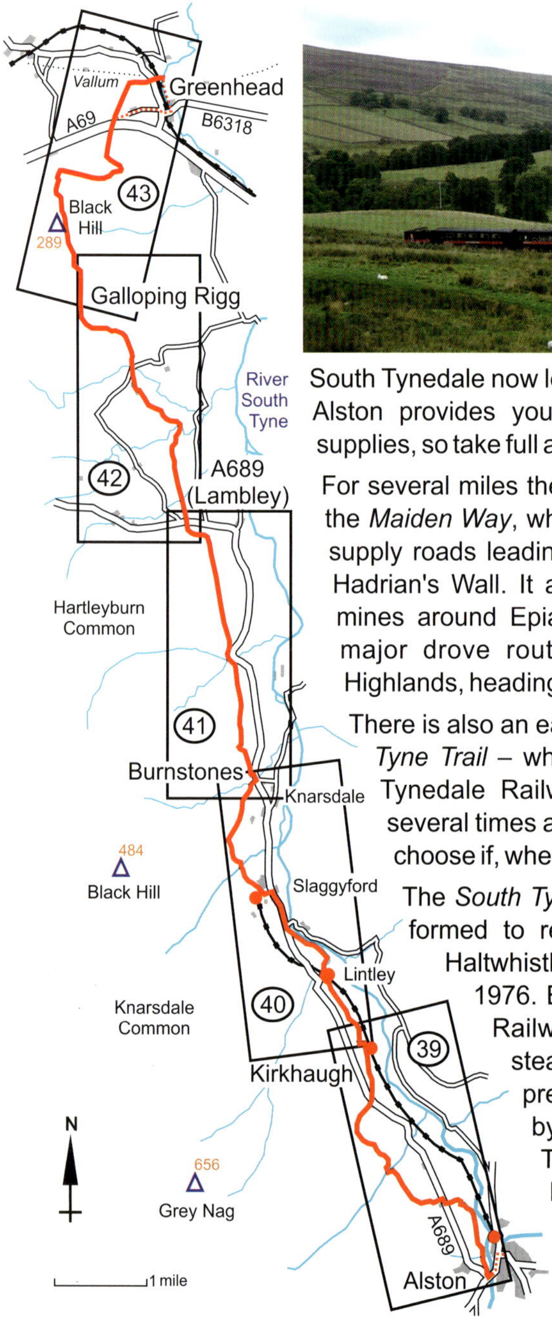

South Tynedale now leads all the way to Hadrian's Wall. Alston provides your last chance to stock up with supplies, so take full advantage of its facilities.

For several miles the Pennine Way follows the line of the *Maiden Way*, which was one of the major Roman supply roads leading from the Stainmore Gap up to Hadrian's Wall. It also serviced the lead and silver mines around Epiacum. Later the road became a major drove route for Scottish cattle from the Highlands, heading south via Teesdale.

There is also an easier alternative route – *the South Tyne Trail* – which follows the line of the South Tynedale Railway. This option presents itself several times along the way, so you can pick and choose if, where or when to take advantage.

The *South Tynedale Preservation Society* was formed to reinstate the line from Alston to Haltwhistle after its closure by British Rail in 1976. By 1983 the new South Tynedale Railway was running narrow gauge steam and diesel trains from Alston. At present they run as far as Lintley, but by 2017 they will reach Slaggyford. The society has ambitious plans to link back to the main line station at Haltwhistle by 2022. That would be a remarkable achievement and provide an incredible community service for the area.

Follow the A686 south from Alston to cross the river and by the War memorial turn right along an access road signed **PW Slaggyford**. The path squeezes along an enclosed track to the left of a house, then across fields to pass around Harbut Lodge and on up to the road by Harbut Law Farm. Just north of the farm the path leaves the road, heading uphill west, following *Isaac's Tea Trail*.

The path climbs the hill, bearing NW before dropping to cross Gilderdale Burn. Climb again to pass Whitlow Farm, curving above the impressive terraces of *Whitley Castle* – the Roman fort of *Epiacum*. It was built around 120 AD, roughly the same time as Hadrian's Wall to which it is linked by the Roman *Maiden Way*.

The path now drops to recross the A689. It cuts across fields heading north, on to Kirkhaugh, where it meets up again with the South Tyne Railway.

If you chose to follow the *South Tyne Trail* alongside the railway line instead, you have saved yourself half a mile (and muddy feet).

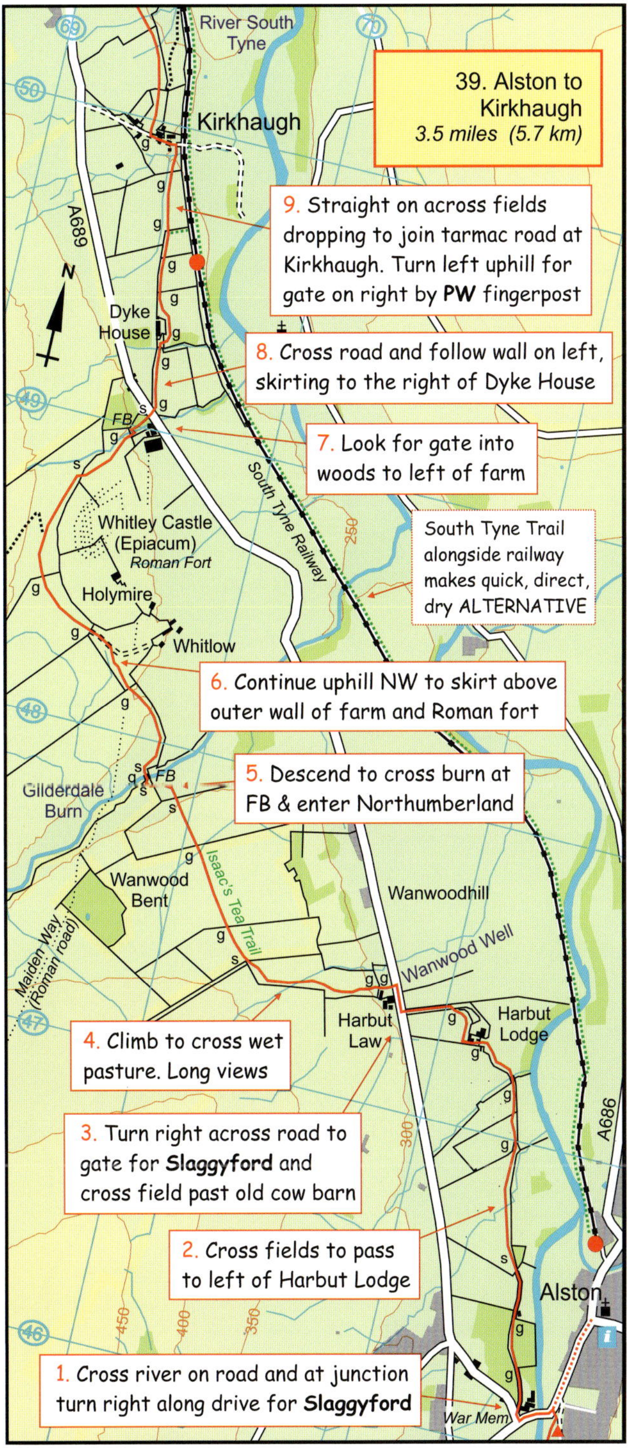

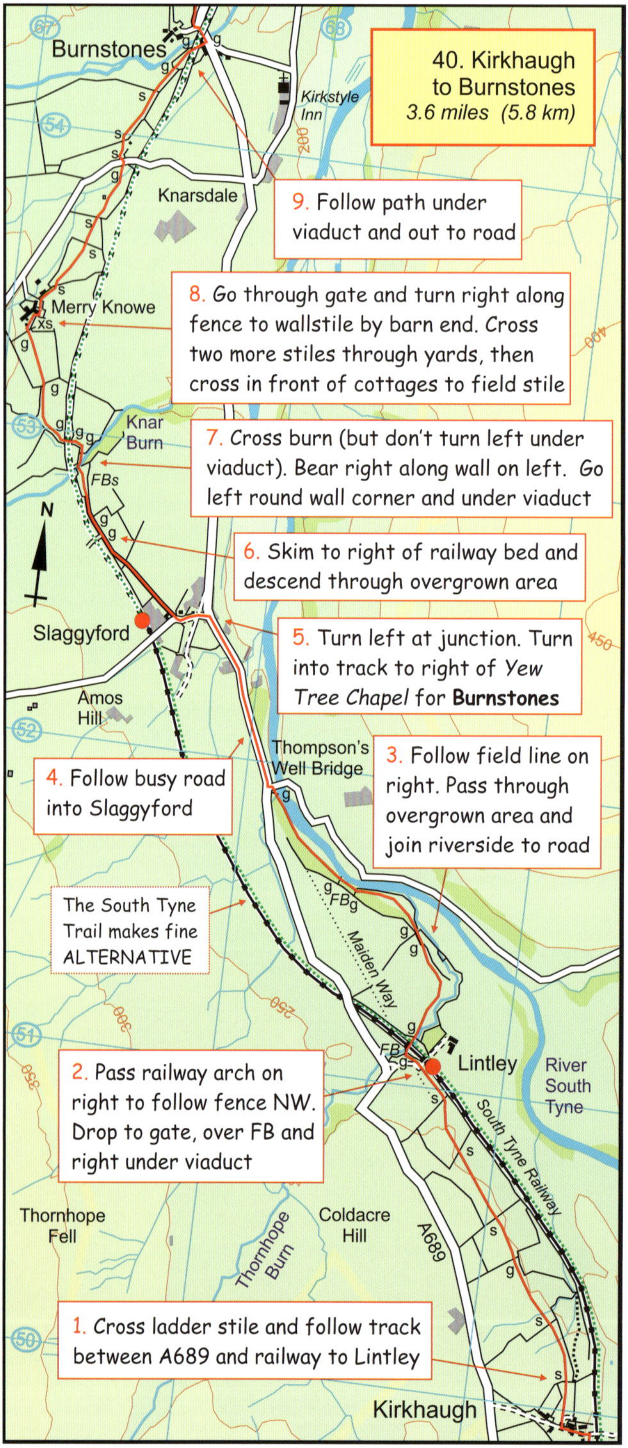

The **Pennine Way** turns left uphill at Kirkhaugh and right through a gate, to continue NW across fields shadowing the railway to the right. It rejoins the railway at Lintley.

Again there is the option to follow the railtrack to Slaggyford, otherwise the **Pennine Way** continues past the railway arch to drop through trees and pass under the railway and across Thornhope Burn, which it follows on the right to join the River South Tyne. It can be overgrown in places here.

At Thompson's Well Bridge turn left and right to follow the A689 into Slaggyford.

Bear left at a junction, uphill, to pass to the right of Yew Tree Chapel for **Burnstones**. The path once again skirts the South Tyne Trail - which could be followed to Burnstones - before cutting down to the right to cross Knar Burn. Care is needed here at a confusion of paths. Don't go immediately under the viaduct but bear right, through a gate and follow a wall on the left to another tunnel under the viaduct.

Now pick up a track that leads up to Merry Knowe, with impressive views backwards across the South Tyne valley. The path turns right, through a series of small yards in front of farm buildings, then on across fields once more to emerge eventually under the viaduct at Burnstones.

The Kirkstyle Inn can be found 300 metres down the minor road eastwards.

Once again there is the option to join the South Tyne Trail on to the magnificent viaduct at Lambley before rejoining the Pennine Way, otherwise turn left onto the access road for **Knarsdale Hall** Estate and go through a corner gate, climbing steeply up a field to join a farm track heading north. The track curves left uphill, where a fingerpost leads back northwards across boggy ground.

The path eventually cuts down to the left to cross Glendue Burn by a kink in the road, then climbs once again, rising over Lambley Common, following the line of the Maiden Way. It is wet in places, but otherwise easy walking, with fine views over the South Tynedale valley. After a mile or so a stile in the fence on the left leads in an arc down to cross the A689 near Lambley.

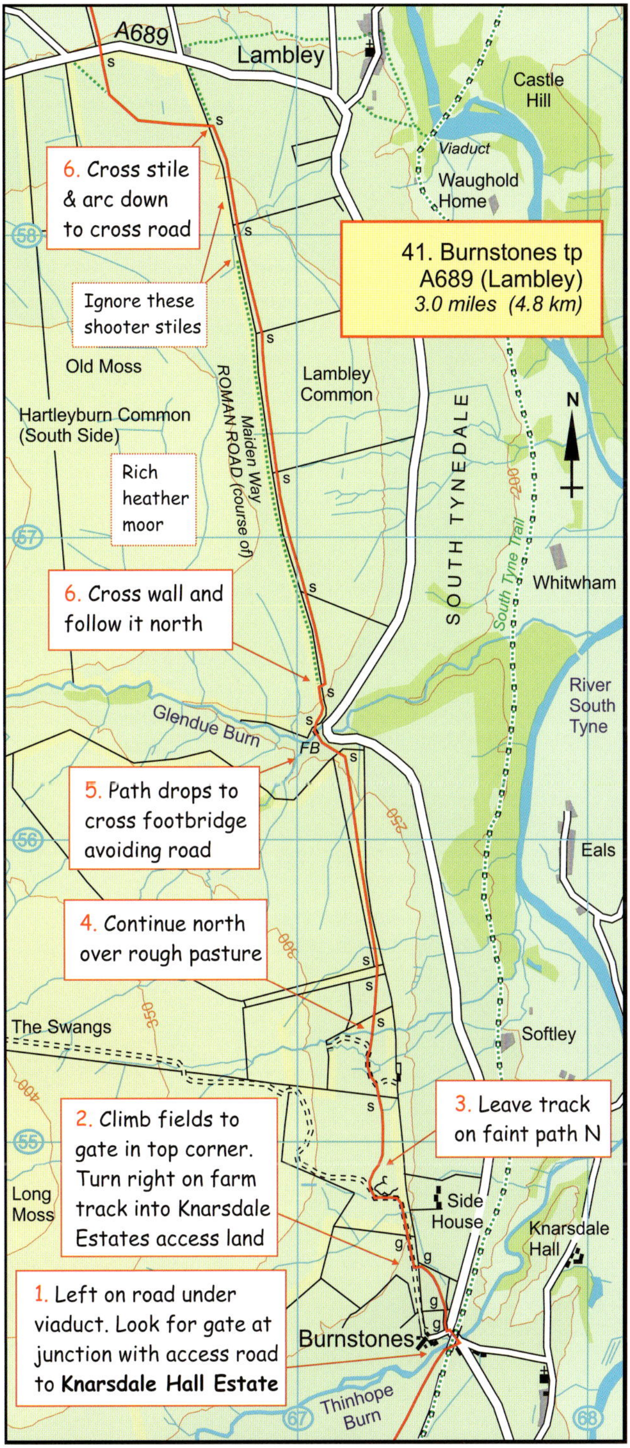

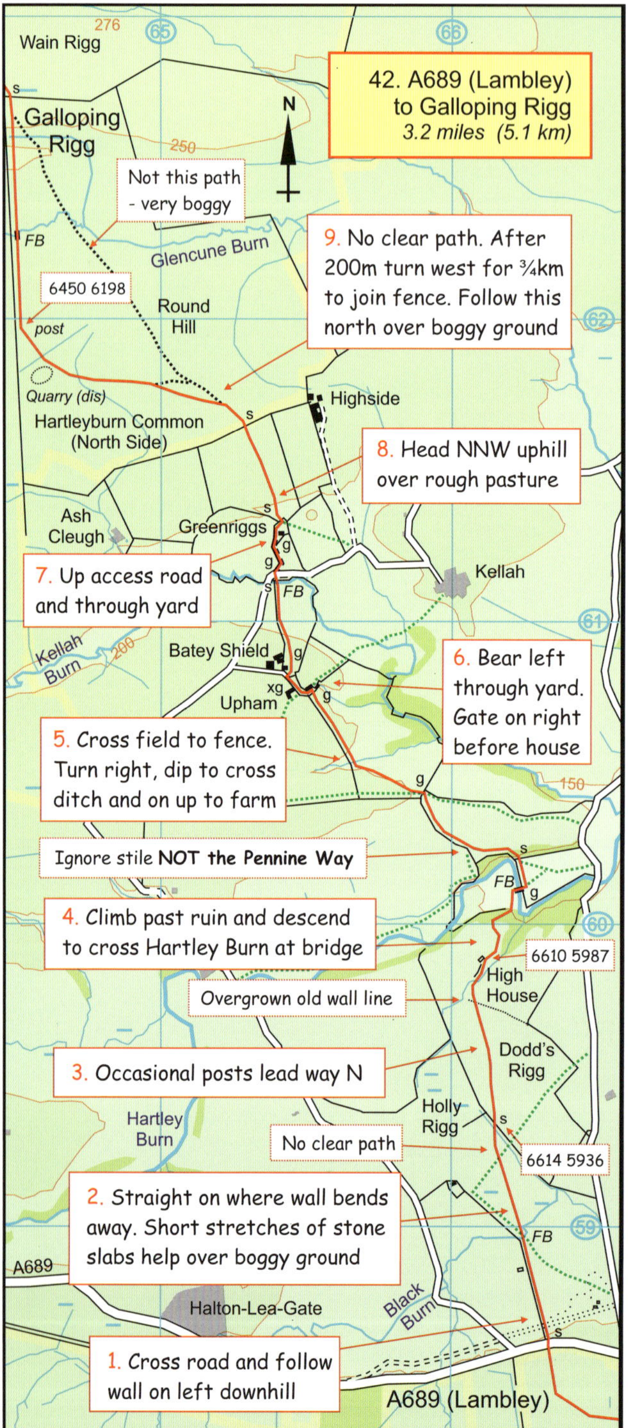

Lambley Viaduct

The best of this section is now behind you, but a further six miles crossing the wetlands of Hartleyburn and Blenkinsopp Commons stretch ahead.

The way continues north, where a faint track and occasional stone slabs lead on to the ruin of High House and across Hartley Burn. The path now curves NW, climbing over farm land to pass through Upham Farm and Greenriggs Farm. Cross the stile at the back of Greenriggs and head straight uphill to another stile, leading out onto open moorland. This is a wild, lonely, desolate place.

Care is needed here in mist, and unless it's been a very dry summer, you should expect to get your feet wet at some point. Continue NW for 200m or so, then bear westwards to eventually locate a fence heading north. Follow this on past the eastern tip of Galloping Rigg to a stile.

Continue northwards, past a fence corner on the left.

Bear NNW, aiming for a wallstile to be found some way to the right of the trig point on the horizon ahead. A boggy path of sorts continues NNW across Black Hill, curving left as it begins to dip to a fence stile, dropping then past two ruined buildings and on to a farm track. Way finding is now easier.

Follow the track east until a fingerpost leads off left along another track curving firstly NW then northwards through trees to cross the very busy A69.

Climb the wooden steps up the bank opposite. If you're heading for Greenhead itself, you can take a shortcut by turning right along the fence to join the old road directly into the village. The Pennine Way continues NNE across fields and alongside a wall with the golf course to your right. Ignore a couple of stiles until you climb a rise to a **Pennine Way** ladder stile by the Roman vallum. Cross the stile and follow the vallum on your left over the golf course, dropping steeply to cross the B6318 under the watchful eye of Thirlwall Castle.

The path crosses the railway line and the Tipal Burn, paths on either side of which can be followed down into Greenhead.

Ahead now lie the splendours of the Roman wall.

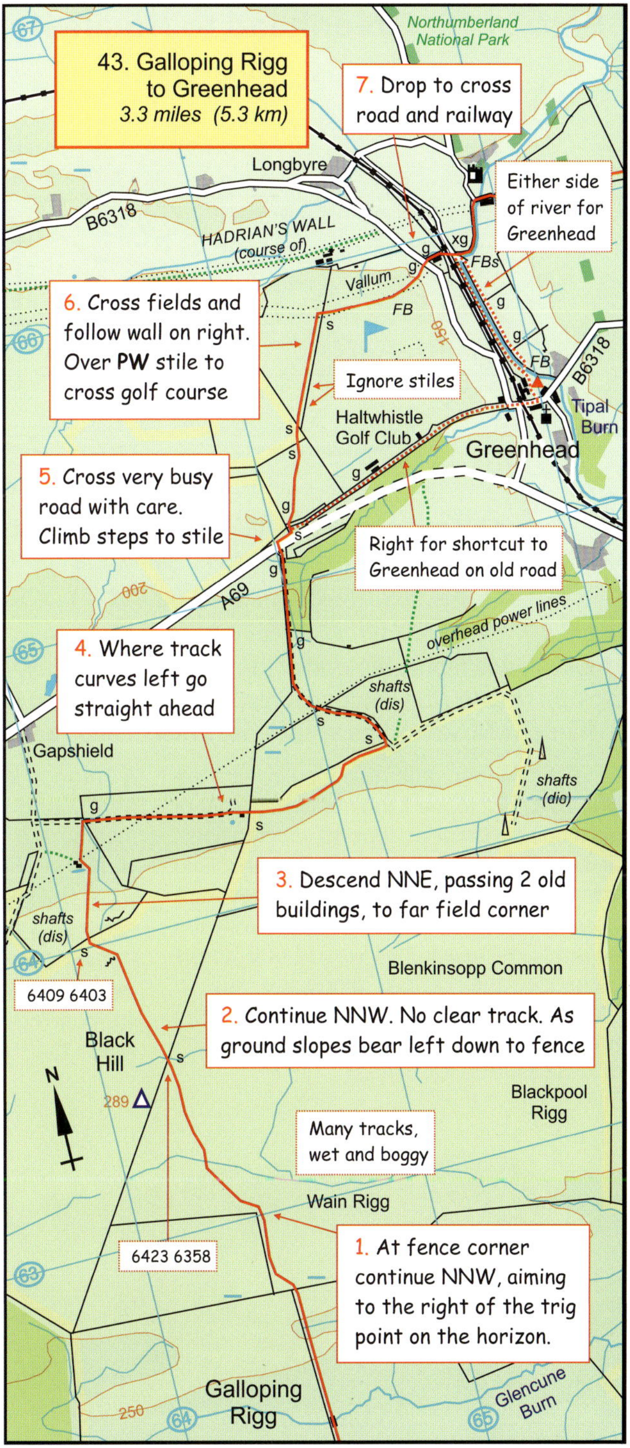

Section 10: **Greenhead to Housesteads & Bardon Mill**

12.9 miles (*20.8 km*)

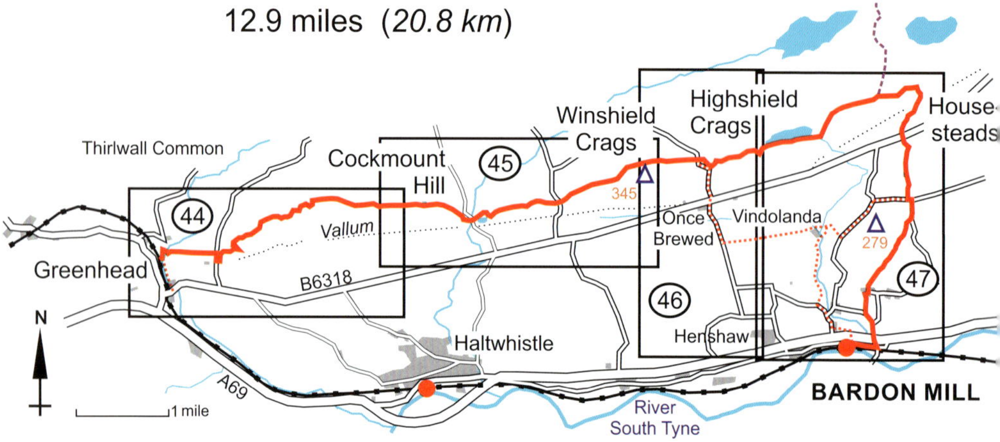

For the next 9½ miles the Pennine Way follows the best preserved (or reconstructed) sections of Hadrian's Wall as it runs along the top of the Whin Sill ridge. It's a rollercoaster ride and though the walking is easy, you will be tired by the time you reach the impressive remains at Housesteads.

Housesteads marks the end of the **Mid Pennine Way**, but unless you've arranged a pick-up or catch the Hadrian's Wall bus, you will need to walk a further 3 miles south to Bardon Mill, which has a mainline railway station and a regular bus service.

Emperor Hadrian ordered the building of the wall in AD 122 to mark the northern border of his empire in Britain. It took 10 years to finish and ran 73 miles (118 km or 80 Roman miles) from Wallsend on Tyne to Bowness-on-Solway. The wall was 4.5m high, with the parapet adding another 2m. 14,000 troops garrisoned the 17 forts along the wall. In between, every Roman mile saw a milecastle with up to 50 auxiliaries, and in between each of these a turret (4 to 8 men).

A 7m wide V-ditch protected the wall to the north, and the broad, bounded vallum marked the southern edge of the military zone. The Military Way supplied the wall.

Hadrian's Wall was finally abandoned in AD 385 as the Romans began to withdraw from Britain. Over the following 1600 years the stone has been plundered and reused in surrounding buildings, churches and farm walls; the 14th century Thirlwall Castle is constructed almost entirely of wall stone, as are many buildings in the town of Haltwhistle.

Walltown Quarry, where the Whin Sill is exposed

Hadrian's Wall became a UNESCO World Heritage Site in 1987 as one of the most complex and well preserved frontiers of the Roman Empire. The 84-mile wall path became Britain's 15th National Trail in 2003.

The line of Hadrian's Wall is rejoined beneath the motte and bailey ruins of Thirlwall Castle. Thirlwall Castle was built in the 1330s by John Thirlwall (Thirlwall means *gap in the wall*) and served to help repel border raiders through the 15th and 16th centuries, after which it fell into disrepair. It is open to the public.

The path climbs steeply uphill alongside the Roman ditch before levelling and the craggy Whin Sill escarpment appears ahead with the first tantalising glimpse of the Roman wall. Turn right on the road and left into the former quarry grounds, now a popular country park with toilets, a visitor centre and refreshments.

Now follows one of the best preserved sections of the wall, along Walltown Crags. **Turret 45A** predates the wall – originally a free standing watchtower later incorporated into the wall. The path dips and climbs, dips and climbs, crossing the hidden bumps of milecastles 45 and 44 before passing through a small plantation and the farm at Cockmount Hill.

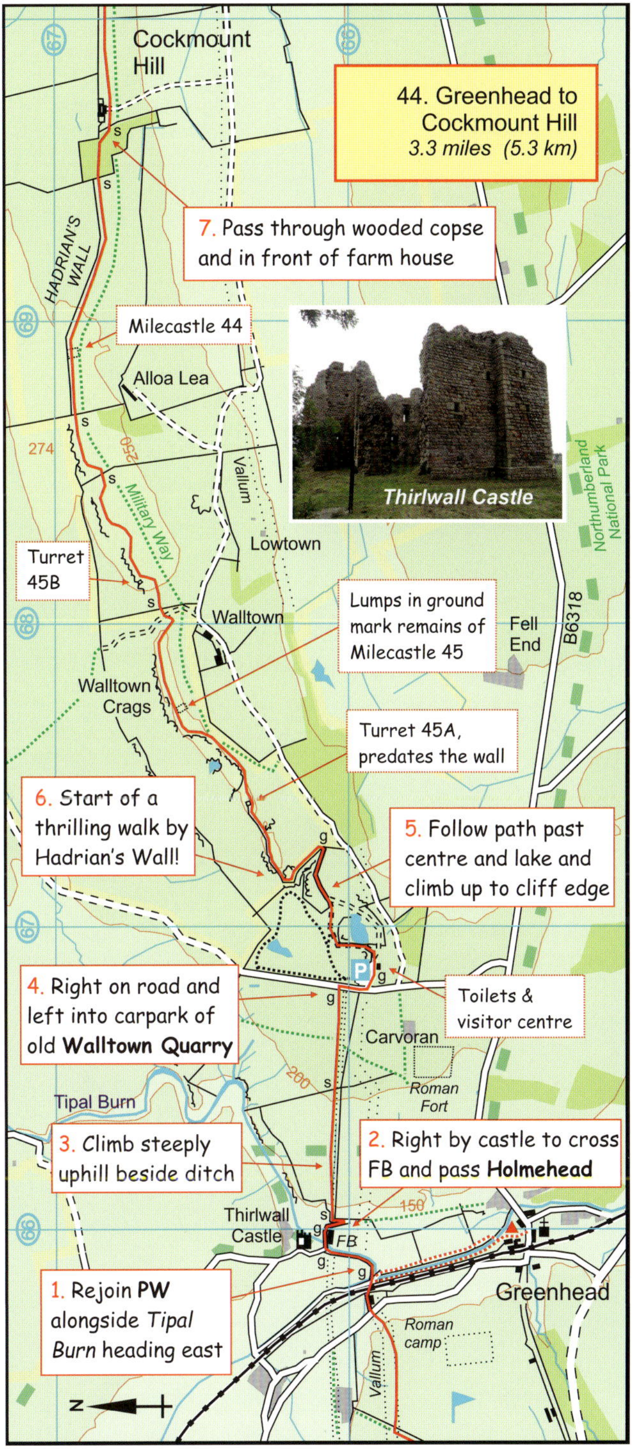

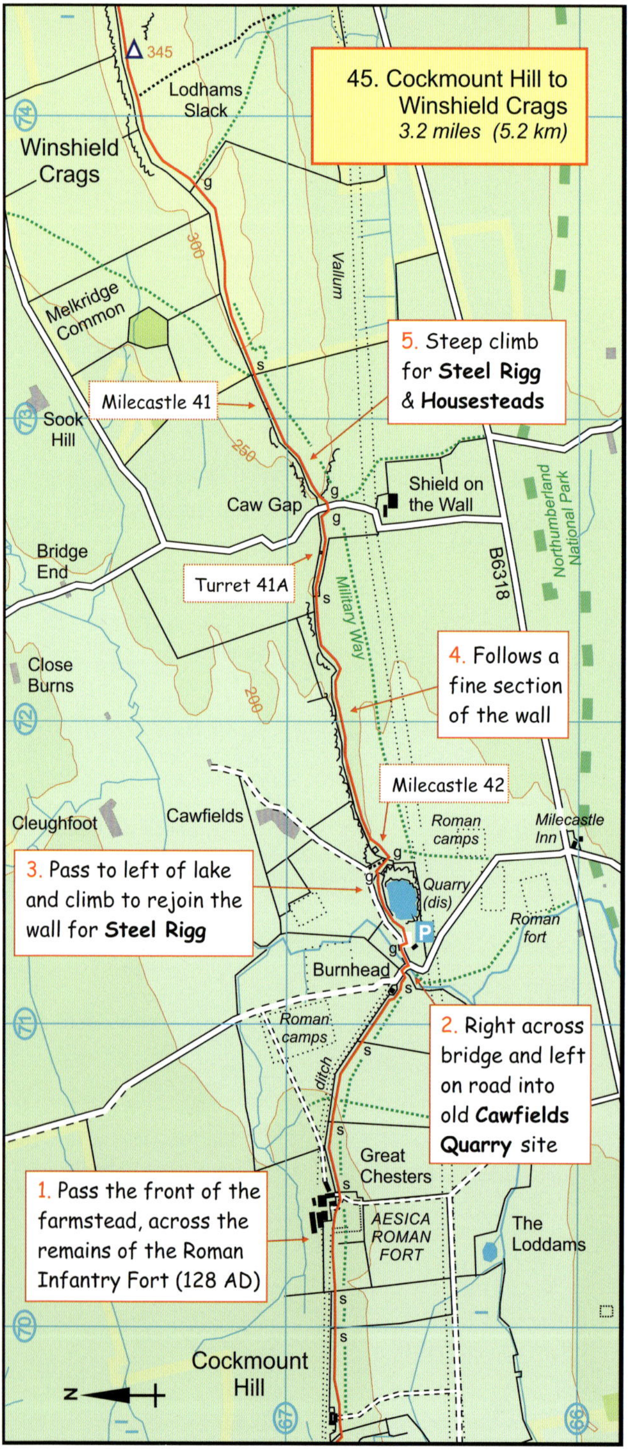

Roman Altar, Great Chesters

Ahead the farm buildings mark the site of the infantry fort of Great Chesters (*Aesica*) which guarded the Caw Gap. It was the last fort to be built, and by the south entrance (along the farm access road) can be seen the only Roman altar still standing along the wall.

The path goes on to join the road at a bridge by the former Cawfields Quarry site, where once again the entire escarpment has been cut through. Quarrying finished in the mid 20th century, the hard rock being used mainly in road building. The popular *Milecastle Inn* can be found half a mile down the road.

There follows another superb section of the wall. Beyond the road at Caw Gap another very steep climb leads eventually to the highest point along the wall at Winshield Crags.

Cawfields Quarry

Approaching Milecastle 39 (top left); Housesteads fort and museum (above left); Communal latrines, south east corner, Housesteads fort (above right); Excavations continue at Vindolanda, with reconstructed wall sections in background (below).

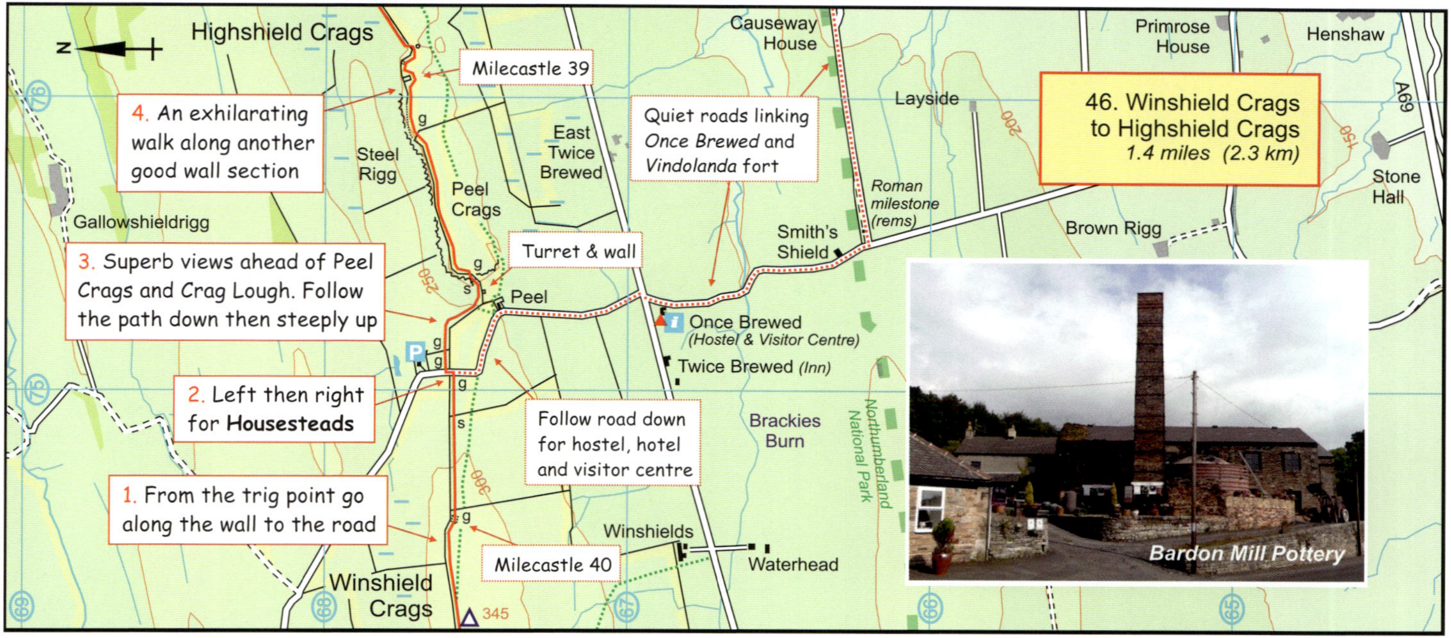

Bardon Mill Pottery

From Winshield Crags the path goes on to pass the car park at Peel. The road can be followed south here for Once or Twice Brewed (National Park Centre, hostel and hotel). The path drops steeply before climbing again onto Peel Crags and one of the most exhilarating sections of the walk. Pass milecastle 39 to climb high above Highshield Crags, where care is needed near the sheer drops to Crag Lough.

The path descends and climbs again above Hotbank Crags, before the Pennine Way proper takes its leave at Rapishaw Gap for the wet moors and packed conifers of Wark Forest - pity those who face a further slog of 13 miles to Bellingham. For **Mid Pennine Way** walkers the climax of the trail - Housesteads - lies just a further half mile on.

Housesteads (*Vercovicium*) is the most complete Roman fort in Britain and makes the perfect end to the Mid Pennine Way. Take time to explore it fully. There's a small museum and giftshop by the southwest corner. It's another 3 miles across moorland directly down to Bardon Mill, or 4 miles if the fascinating fort excavation and museum at *Vindolanda* is included. The National Park Centre at Once Brewed can be incorporated into a popular circular walk. Enjoy the end of the walk, and well done!

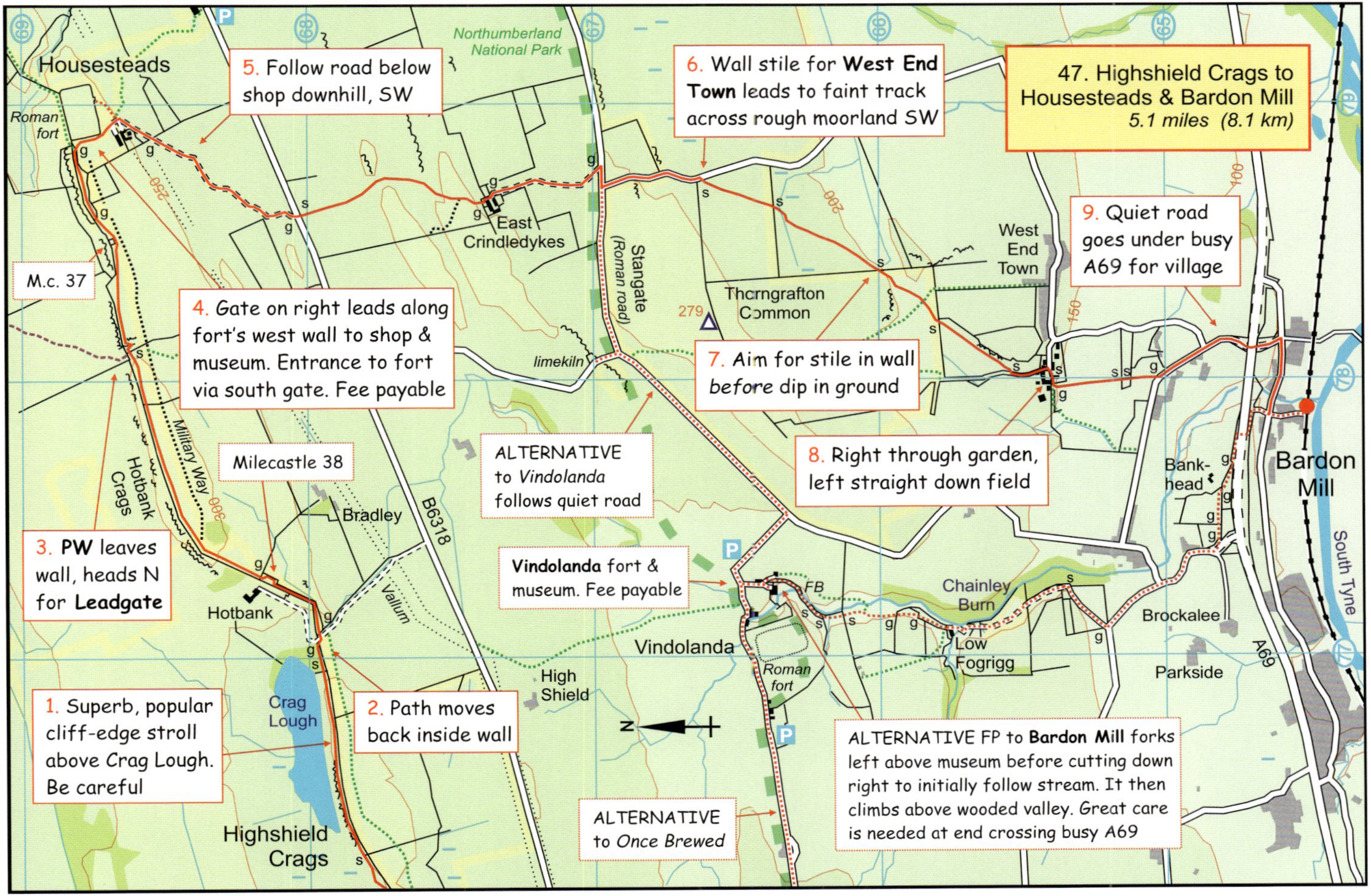
47. Highshield Crags to Housesteads & Bardon Mill
5.1 miles (8.1 km)
1. Superb, popular cliff-edge stroll above Crag Lough. Be careful
2. Path moves back inside wall
3. PW leaves wall, heads N for Leadgate
4. Gate on right leads along fort's west wall to shop & museum. Entrance to fort via south gate. Fee payable
5. Follow road below shop downhill, SW
6. Wall stile for West End Town leads to faint track across rough moorland SW
7. Aim for stile in wall before dip in ground
8. Right through garden, left straight down field
9. Quiet road goes under busy A69 for village
ALTERNATIVE to Vindolanda follows quiet road
Vindolanda fort & museum. Fee payable
ALTERNATIVE to Once Brewed
ALTERNATIVE FP to Bardon Mill forks left above museum before cutting down right to initially follow stream. It then climbs above wooded valley. Great care is needed at end crossing busy A69
Milecastle 38
M.c. 37
Housesteads
Roman fort
Northumberland National Park
East Crindledykes
Stangate (Roman road)
limekiln
Thorngrafton Common
279
West End Town
Bardon Mill
Bankhead
Brockalee
Parkside
South Tyne
A69
Chainley Burn
Low Fogrigg
FB
Vindolanda
Roman fort
High Shield
Bradley
B6318
Vallum
Military Way
Hotbank Crags
Hotbank
Crag Lough
Highshield Crags
N

APPENDIX: UNFINISHED BUSINESS

PW SOUTH: Edale to Calder Valley 42.5 miles *(68.4 km)*

The two end stages of the Pennine Way are undoubtedly the toughest both physically and logistically. They favour backpackers who carry everything they need. Accommodation and facilities are scarce, often involving detours off route. As distinct stages of three or four days they each become much more manageable. Mapped here at a scale of 1:50,000.

The Pennine Way starts from the Old Nag's Head in the lovely Derbyshire village of Edale, which is easily accessible by mainline rail from Sheffield or Manchester. This stage is usually tackled in three days, with breaks at Torside and Standedge; in both cases accommodation must be sought off route unless camping.

The modern ascent of Kinder Scout is quite straight forward though steep and there's little danger of getting lost along the gritstone edges of the plateau. The route across Featherbed Moss is flagged all the way. Beyond Snake Pass some care is needed in mist crossing Bleaklow. The descent along Torside Clough is long and tiring, though offering excellent views.

The climb above Laddow Rocks is another highlight, though care is again needed in mist crossing Black Hill. Then begins a lengthy stretch alongside reservoirs at Wessenden. Some walkers cut off for Marsden whilst the Pennine Way heads up to the A62 at Standedge.

The third day involves an unpleasant moorland trek squeezed between the noisy conurbations of Lancashire and West Yorkshire, to cross the M62. The climb along the gritstone outcrop of Blackstone Edge is memorable, leading to the Aiggin Stone and the cobbled Roman road. A long spell of easy walking alongside more reservoirs eventually brings the distinctive Stoodley Pike into view. The Pennine Way crosses the Calder Valley a mile to the west of Hebden Bridge, but the new Loop route presents the option of enjoying all that this lively mill town has to offer.

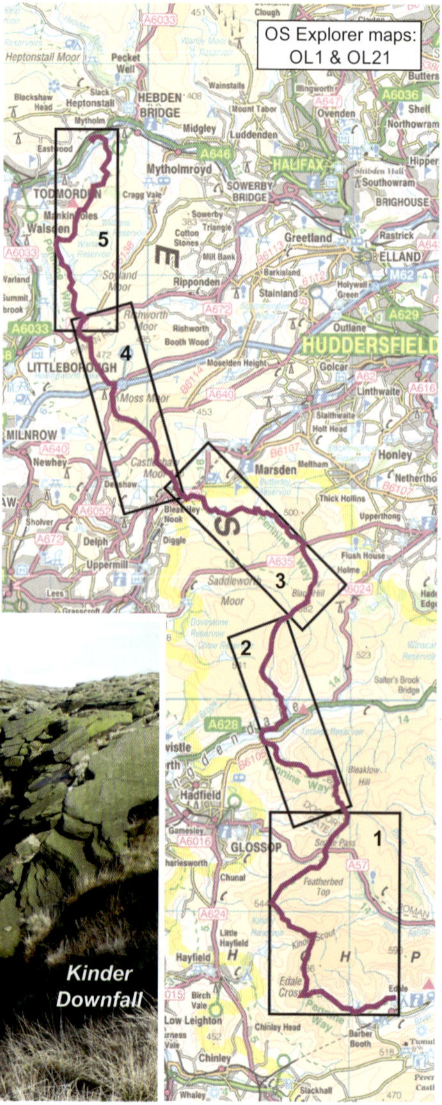

Kinder Downfall

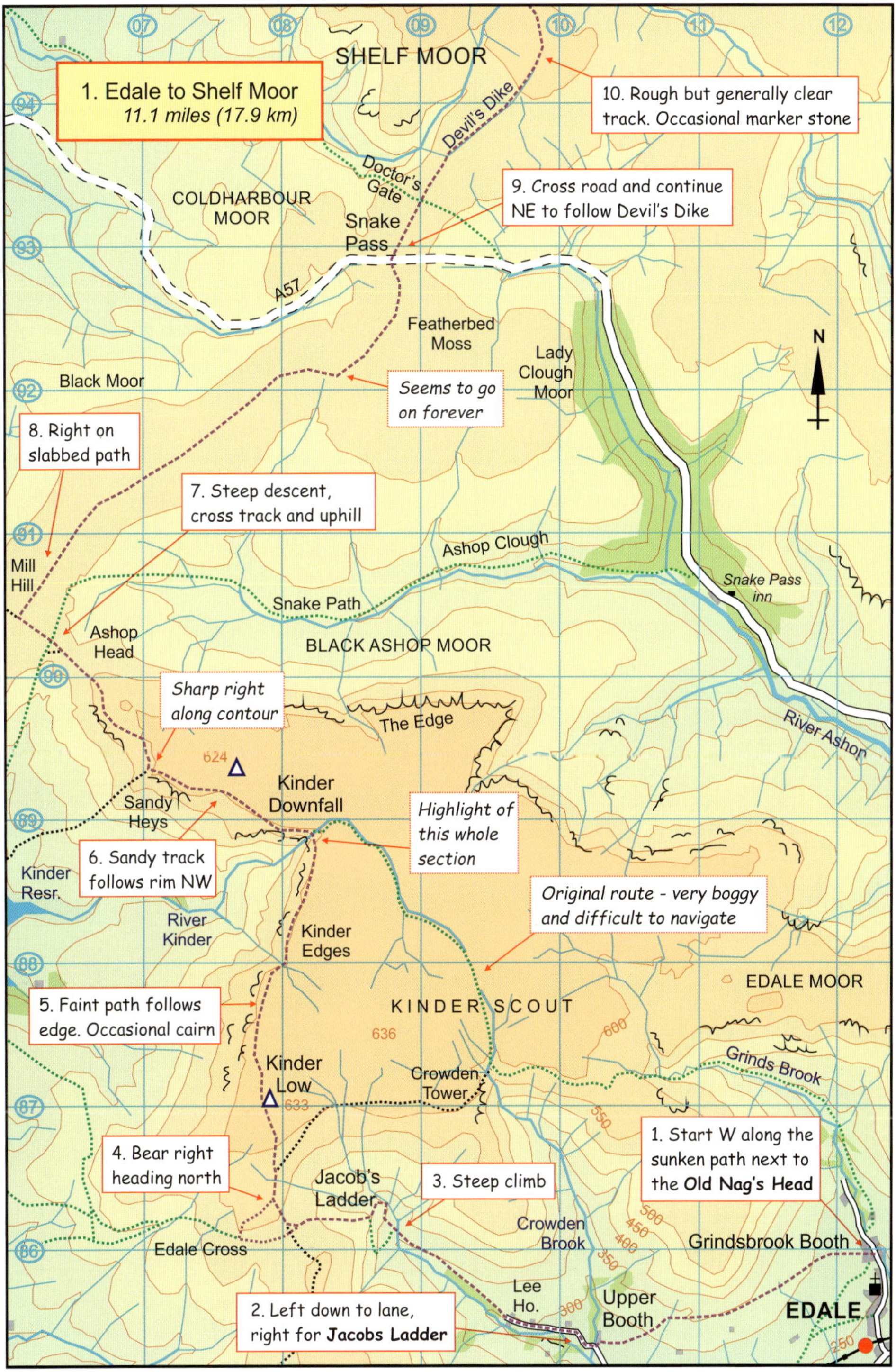

1. Edale to Shelf Moor
11.1 miles (17.9 km)
SHELF MOOR
COLDHARBOUR MOOR
Snake Pass
Doctor's Gate
Devil's Dike
A57
Featherbed Moss
Lady Clough Moor
Black Moor
Mill Hill
Ashop Head
Ashop Clough
Snake Path
BLACK ASHOP MOOR
Snake Pass inn
River Ashop
The Edge
Kinder Downfall
Sandy Heys
Kinder Resr.
River Kinder
Kinder Edges
KINDER SCOUT
EDALE MOOR
Grinds Brook
Kinder Low
Crowden Tower
Jacob's Ladder
Edale Cross
Crowden Brook
Lee Ho.
Upper Booth
Grindsbrook Booth
EDALE
N
10. Rough but generally clear track. Occasional marker stone
9. Cross road and continue NE to follow Devil's Dike
Seems to go on forever
8. Right on slabbed path
7. Steep descent, cross track and uphill
Sharp right along contour
6. Sandy track follows rim NW
Highlight of this whole section
Original route - very boggy and difficult to navigate
5. Faint path follows edge. Occasional cairn
4. Bear right heading north
3. Steep climb
1. Start W along the sunken path next to the Old Nag's Head
2. Left down to lane, right for Jacobs Ladder

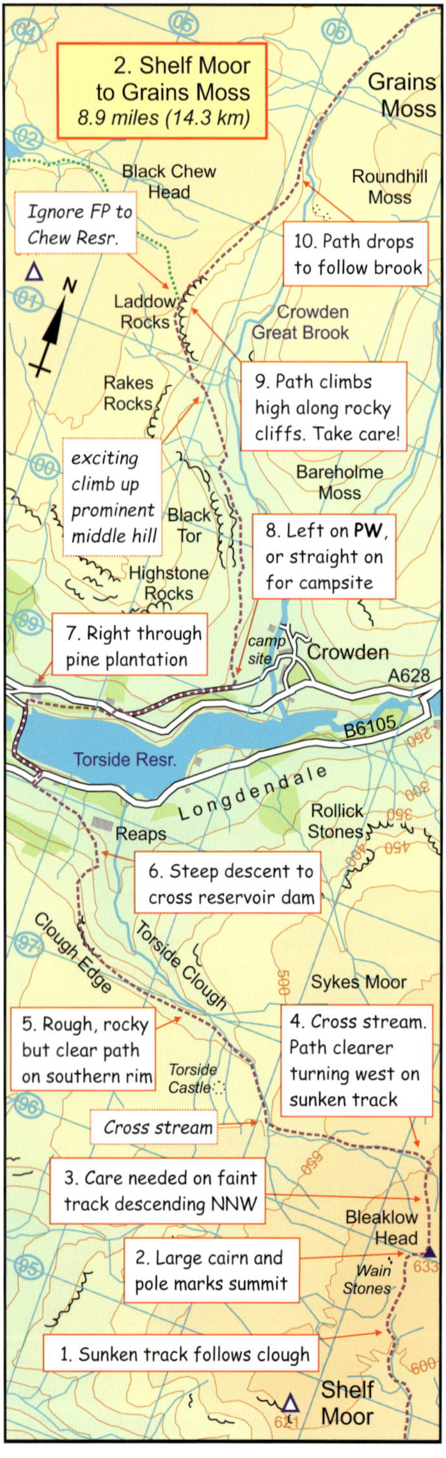
2. Shelf Moor to Grains Moss
8.9 miles (14.3 km)
Grains Moss
Black Chew Head
Roundhill Moss
Ignore FP to Chew Resr.
10. Path drops to follow brook
Laddow Rocks
Crowden Great Brook
Rakes Rocks
9. Path climbs high along rocky cliffs. Take care!
exciting climb up prominent middle hill
Bareholme Moss
Black Tor
8. Left on PW, or straight on for campsite
Highstone Rocks
7. Right through pine plantation
camp site
Crowden
A628
B6105
Torside Resr.
Longdendale
Rollick Stones
Reaps
6. Steep descent to cross reservoir dam
Clough Edge
Torside Clough
Sykes Moor
5. Rough, rocky but clear path on southern rim
Torside Castle
4. Cross stream. Path clearer turning west on sunken track
Cross stream
3. Care needed on faint track descending NNW
Bleaklow Head
633
2. Large cairn and pole marks summit
Wain Stones
1. Sunken track follows clough
Shelf Moor
621

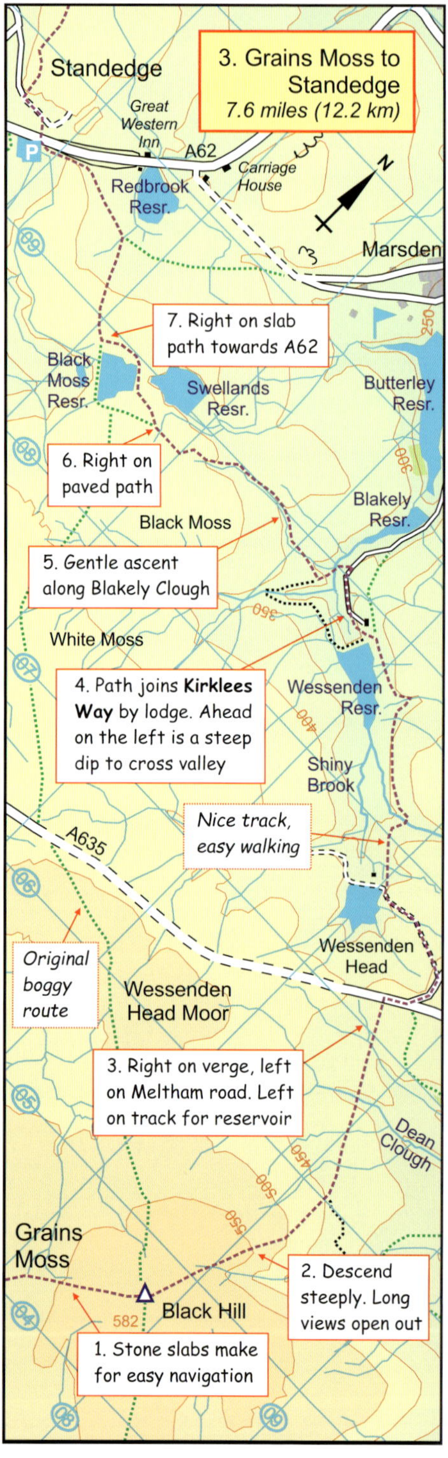
3. Grains Moss to Standedge
7.6 miles (12.2 km)
Standedge
Great Western Inn
A62
Carriage House
Redbrook Resr.
Marsden
7. Right on slab path towards A62
Black Moss Resr.
Swellands Resr.
Butterley Resr.
6. Right on paved path
Blakely Resr.
Black Moss
5. Gentle ascent along Blakely Clough
White Moss
4. Path joins Kirklees Way by lodge. Ahead on the left is a steep dip to cross valley
Wessenden Resr.
Shiny Brook
Nice track, easy walking
A635
Wessenden Head
Original boggy route
Wessenden Head Moor
3. Right on verge, left on Meltham road. Left on track for reservoir
Dean Clough
Grains Moss
2. Descend steeply. Long views open out
Black Hill
582
1. Stone slabs make for easy navigation

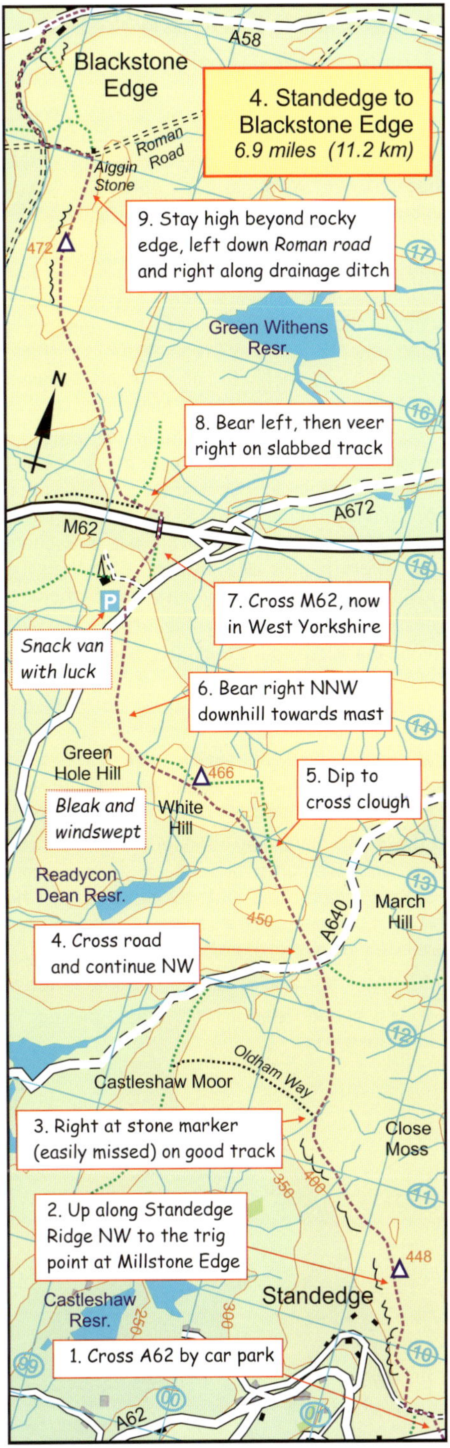

4. Standedge to Blackstone Edge
6.9 miles (11.2 km)
Blackstone Edge
A58
Roman Road
Aiggin Stone
9. Stay high beyond rocky edge, left down Roman road and right along drainage ditch
472
Green Withens Resr.
N
8. Bear left, then veer right on slabbed track
M62
A672
7. Cross M62, now in West Yorkshire
Snack van with luck
6. Bear right NNW downhill towards mast
Green Hole Hill
White Hill
466
Bleak and windswept
5. Dip to cross clough
Readycon Dean Resr.
450
A640
March Hill
4. Cross road and continue NW
Castleshaw Moor
Oldham Way
3. Right at stone marker (easily missed) on good track
Close Moss
350
400
2. Up along Standedge Ridge NW to the trig point at Millstone Edge
448
Castleshaw Resr.
250
300
Standedge
1. Cross A62 by car park
A62

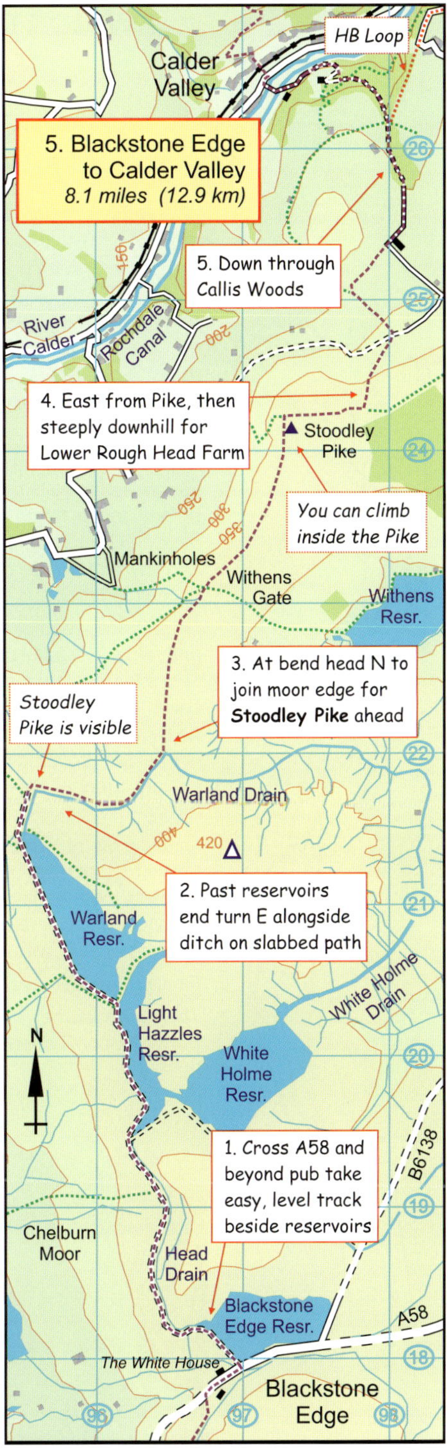

HB Loop
Calder Valley
5. Blackstone Edge to Calder Valley
8.1 miles (12.9 km)
150
5. Down through Callis Woods
River Calder
Rochdale Canal
200
4. East from Pike, then steeply downhill for Lower Rough Head Farm
Stoodley Pike
You can climb inside the Pike
250
300
350
Mankinholes
Withens Gate
Withens Resr.
3. At bend head N to join moor edge for Stoodley Pike ahead
Stoodley Pike is visible
Warland Drain
400
420
2. Past reservoirs end turn E alongside ditch on slabbed path
Warland Resr.
Light Hazzles Resr.
White Holme Resr.
White Holme Drain
N
1. Cross A58 and beyond pub take easy, level track beside reservoirs
B6138
Chelburn Moor
Head Drain
Blackstone Edge Resr.
A58
The White House
Blackstone Edge

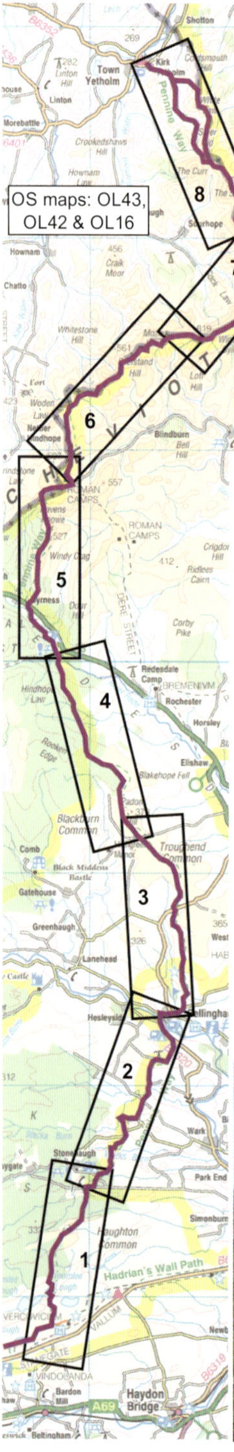

PW NORTH: Hadrian's Wall to Kirk Yetholm

53.1 miles *(85.4 km)*

The final stage at the northern end of the Pennine Way usually takes 3 or 4 days, dependant on how you tackle the long stretch across the Cheviots. The 27 mile walk along the Cheviot ridge is without doubt the highlight of this stage, but to get there involves a somewhat tedious two day trek across wet moorland and the thick pine plantations of the Kielder Forest.

The Pennine Way leaves Hadrian's Wall at Rapishaw Gap, half a mile west of Housesteads. It heads north to pass quickly through the eastern fringes of Wark Forest, then meanders across farmland to reach Shitlington Crags. A brief moorland crossing brings you finally to the Northumberland market town of Bellingham and definitely your last chance to restock.

The next day starts with more damp moorland, crossing Hareshaw Common, before a minor ridge walk of sorts brings you to Padon Hill. There follows a boggy stretch, skirting Redesdale Forest before relief is found on the firm but very long forest track. The forest is these days much less oppressive than it once was. Finally the River Rede is reached, and the tiny village of Byrness, where there's little more on offer than the accommodation and facilities at the *Forest View Walkers Inn* or *The Byrness*.

Given good weather the Cheviot ridge walk is a sheer delight, but hard wind and rain will quickly take its toll on the exposed fell tops. Two wooden refuge huts offer the only respite. With a very early start and sunshine it's possible to cover the 27 miles in one go, given that it's the last day. Many people though arrange a pick-up with their accommodation providers to break this section half way, either dropping from Windy Gyle to the Coquet valley east, or taking the ancient Clennel Street track down to Cocklawfoot in the west. Either way involves a 2½ mile descent, and obviously a climb back up the following day.

Once up on the ridge the path makes for quite easy walking, with stone slabs taking care of most boggy areas. Once the border fence is joined there's little problem route finding. There's a significant climb up to the junction with the Cheviot itself, where a decision must be made. There's a final choice of routes down at the end, with the more modern high level route being preferred.

Finally, there's the walk into Kirk Yetholm and a celebration at the Border Hotel.

The return journey home involves a bus to Kelso and from there another to Berwick-upon-Tweed or Edinburgh for trains.

Cheviots

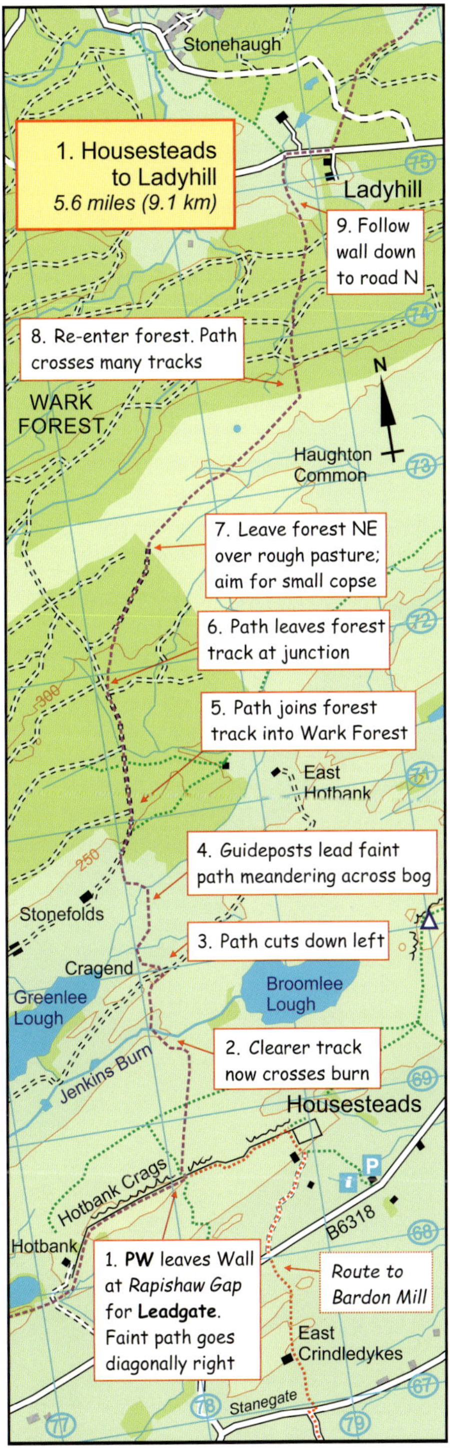

1. Housesteads to Ladyhill
5.6 miles (9.1 km)
Stonehaugh
Ladyhill
9. Follow wall down to road N
8. Re-enter forest. Path crosses many tracks
WARK FOREST
N
Haughton Common
7. Leave forest NE over rough pasture; aim for small copse
6. Path leaves forest track at junction
300
5. Path joins forest track into Wark Forest
East Hotbank
250
4. Guideposts lead faint path meandering across bog
Stonefolds
3. Path cuts down left
Cragend
Greenlee Lough
Broomlee Lough
2. Clearer track now crosses burn
Jenkins Burn
Housesteads
Hotbank Crags
Hotbank
B6318
1. PW leaves Wall at Rapishaw Gap for Leadgate. Faint path goes diagonally right
Route to Bardon Mill
East Crindledykes
Stanegate

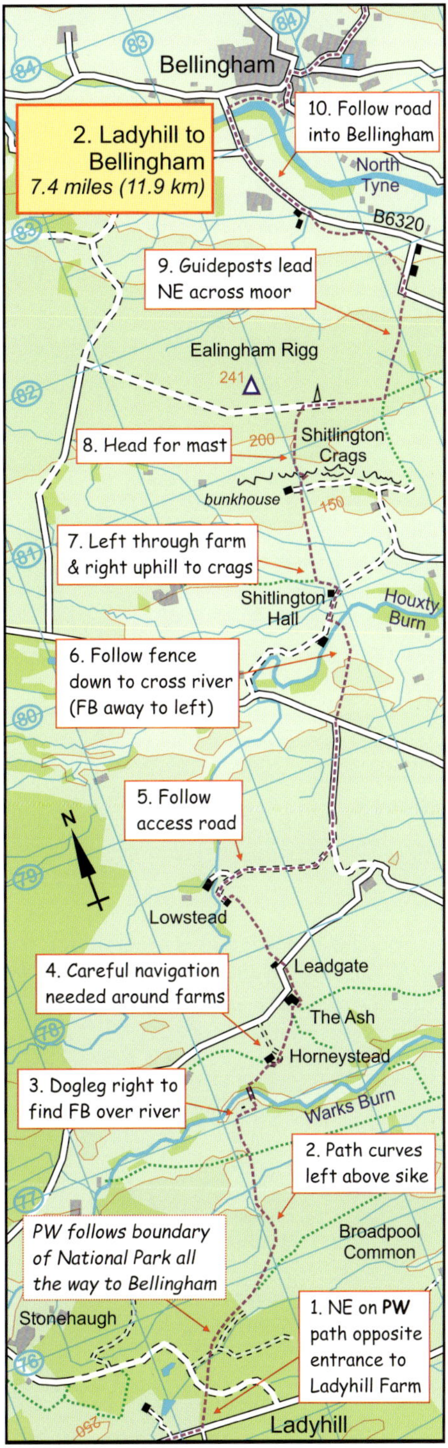

Bellingham
2. Ladyhill to Bellingham
7.4 miles (11.9 km)
10. Follow road into Bellingham
North Tyne
B6320
9. Guideposts lead NE across moor
Ealingham Rigg
241
8. Head for mast
200
Shitlington Crags
bunkhouse
150
7. Left through farm & right uphill to crags
Shitlington Hall
Houxty Burn
6. Follow fence down to cross river (FB away to left)
5. Follow access road
N
Lowstead
4. Careful navigation needed around farms
Leadgate
The Ash
Horneystead
3. Dogleg right to find FB over river
Warks Burn
2. Path curves left above sike
Broadpool Common
PW follows boundary of National Park all the way to Bellingham
Stonehaugh
1. NE on PW path opposite entrance to Ladyhill Farm
Ladyhill

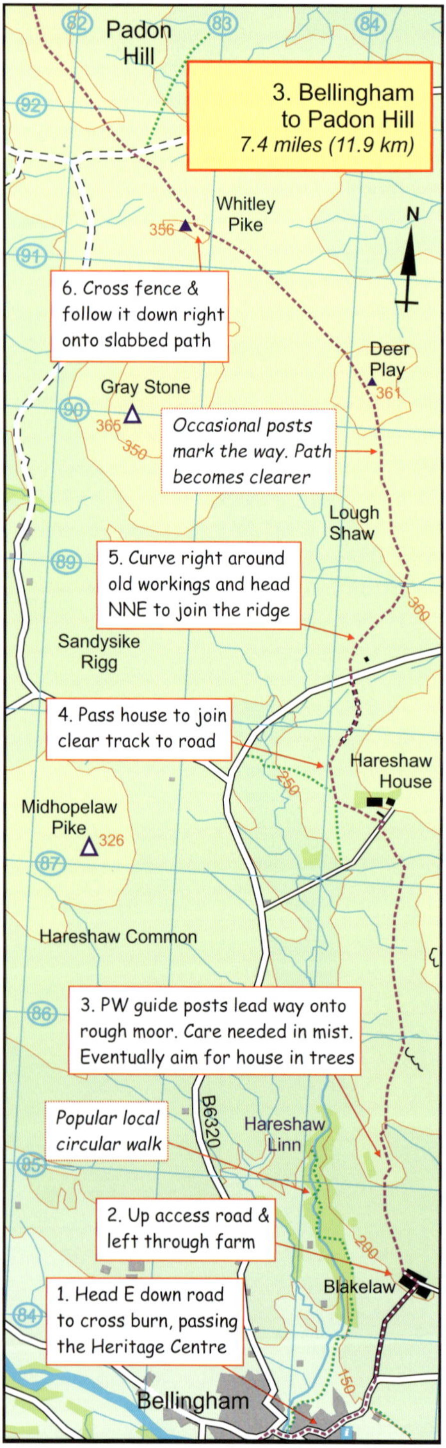
3. Bellingham to Padon Hill
7.4 miles (11.9 km)
Padon Hill
Whitley Pike
356
6. Cross fence & follow it down right onto slabbed path
Deer Play
361
Gray Stone
365
350
Occasional posts mark the way. Path becomes clearer
Lough Shaw
5. Curve right around old workings and head NNE to join the ridge
300
Sandysike Rigg
4. Pass house to join clear track to road
Hareshaw House
250
Midhopelaw Pike
326
Hareshaw Common
3. PW guide posts lead way onto rough moor. Care needed in mist. Eventually aim for house in trees
Popular local circular walk
B6320
Hareshaw Linn
2. Up access road & left through farm
200
Blakelaw
1. Head E down road to cross burn, passing the Heritage Centre
150
Bellingham
N
82
83
84
92
91
90
89
87
86
85
84

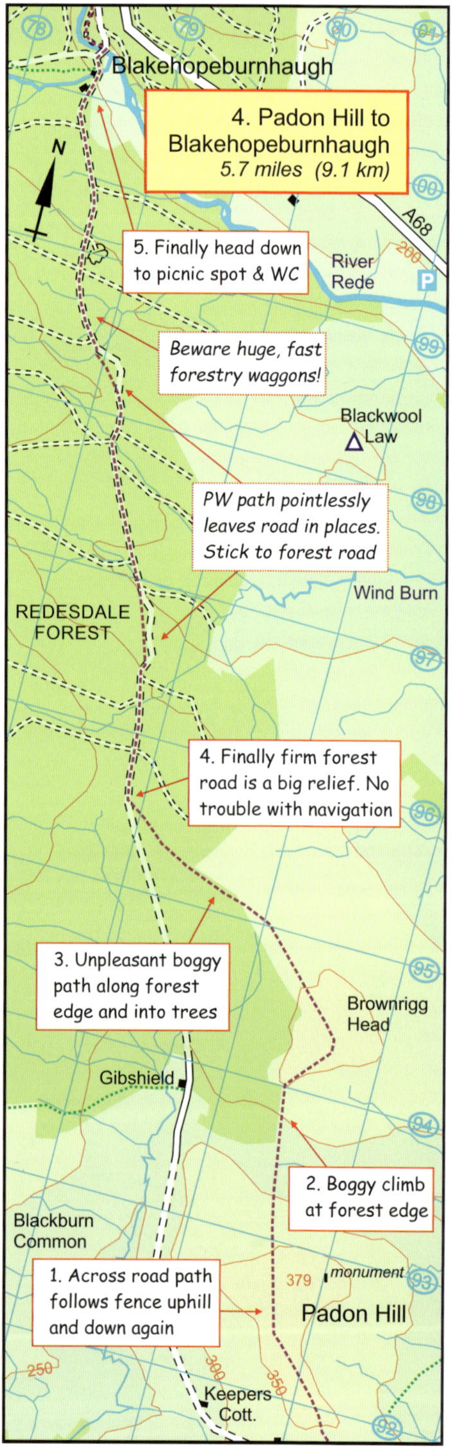
Blakehopeburnhaugh
4. Padon Hill to Blakehopeburnhaugh
5.7 miles (9.1 km)
A68
5. Finally head down to picnic spot & WC
River Rede
200
P
Beware huge, fast forestry waggons!
Blackwool Law
PW path pointlessly leaves road in places. Stick to forest road
Wind Burn
REDESDALE FOREST
4. Finally firm forest road is a big relief. No trouble with navigation
3. Unpleasant boggy path along forest edge and into trees
Brownrigg Head
Gibshield
2. Boggy climb at forest edge
Blackburn Common
1. Across road path follows fence uphill and down again
379
monument
Padon Hill
250
300
350
Keepers Cott.
N
78
79
80
81
00
99
98
97
96
95
94
93
92

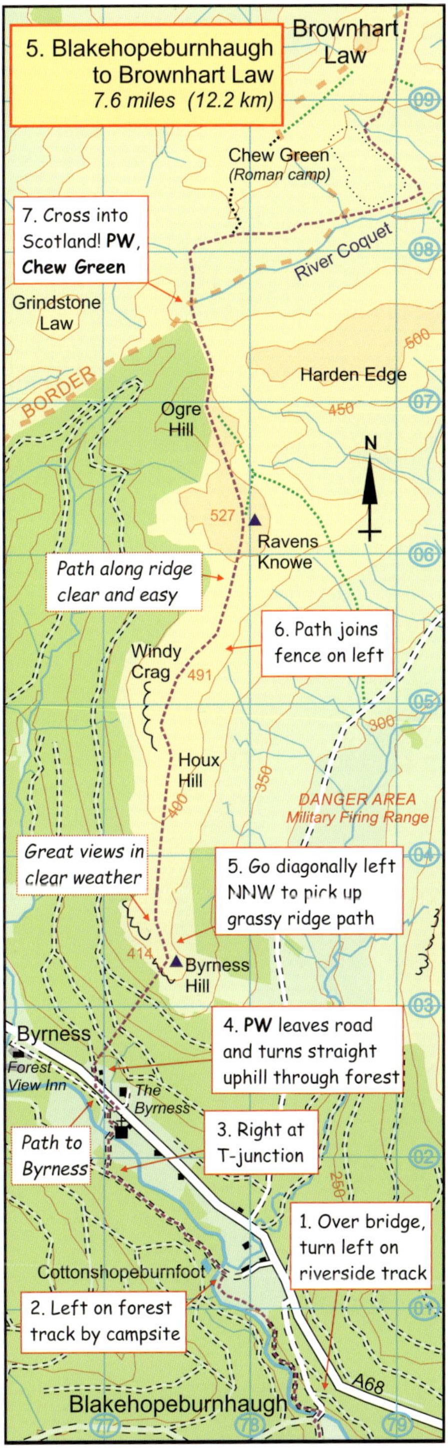

5. Blakehopeburnhaugh to Brownhart Law
7.6 miles (12.2 km)
Brownhart Law
Chew Green
(Roman camp)
7. Cross into Scotland! PW, Chew Green
River Coquet
Grindstone Law
BORDER
Harden Edge
Ogre Hill
N
Ravens Knowe
Path along ridge clear and easy
6. Path joins fence on left
Windy Crag
Houx Hill
DANGER AREA
Military Firing Range
Great views in clear weather
5. Go diagonally left NNW to pick up grassy ridge path
Byrness Hill
Byrness
Forest View Inn
The Byrness
4. PW leaves road and turns straight uphill through forest
Path to Byrness
3. Right at T-junction
1. Over bridge, turn left on riverside track
Cottonshopeburnfoot
2. Left on forest track by campsite
A68
Blakehopeburnhaugh

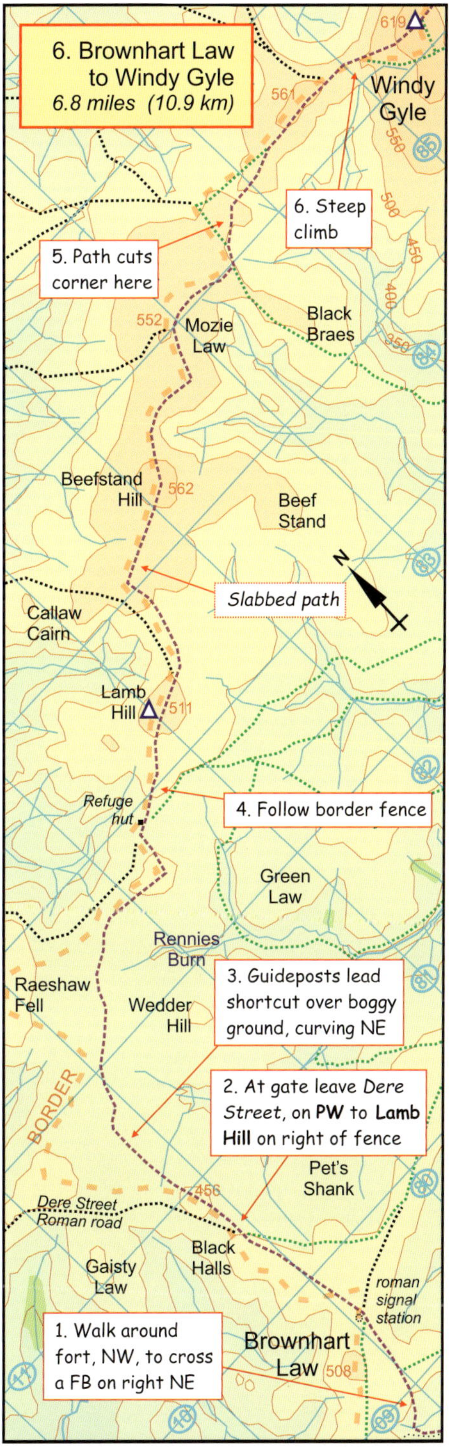

6. Brownhart Law to Windy Gyle
6.8 miles (10.9 km)
Windy Gyle
6. Steep climb
5. Path cuts corner here
Mozie Law
Black Braes
Beefstand Hill
Beef Stand
N
Slabbed path
Callaw Cairn
Lamb Hill
Refuge hut
4. Follow border fence
Green Law
Rennies Burn
Raeshaw Fell
Wedder Hill
3. Guideposts lead shortcut over boggy ground, curving NE
2. At gate leave Dere Street, on PW to Lamb Hill on right of fence
BORDER
Pet's Shank
Dere Street
Roman road
Black Halls
Gaisty Law
roman signal station
1. Walk around fort, NW, to cross a FB on right NE
Brownhart Law

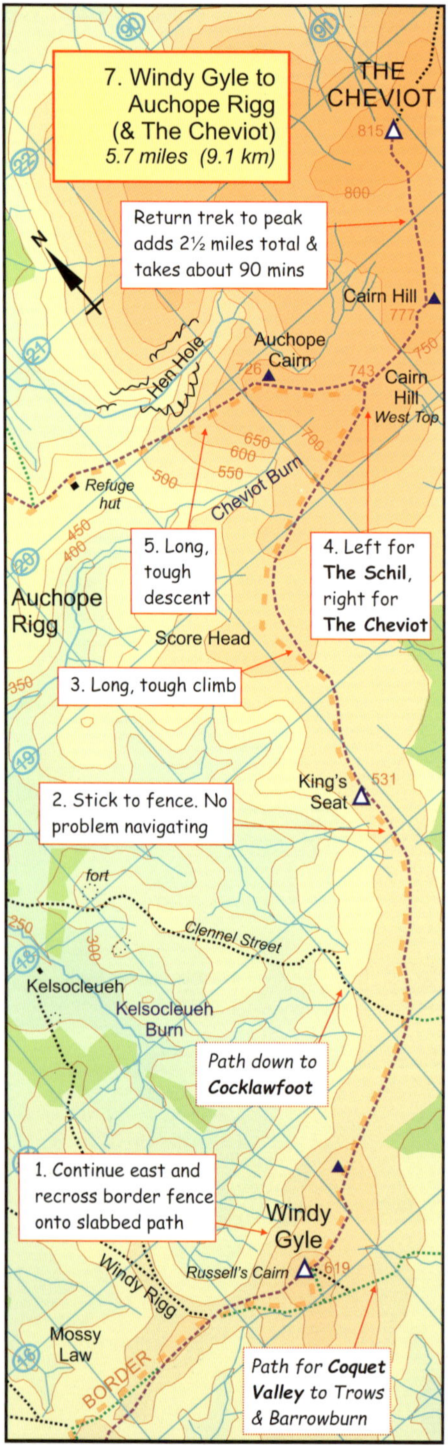
7. Windy Gyle to Auchope Rigg (& The Cheviot)
5.7 miles (9.1 km)
THE CHEVIOT
815
800
Return trek to peak adds 2½ miles total & takes about 90 mins
N
Cairn Hill
777
750
Auchope Cairn
726
743
Cairn Hill West Top
Hen Hole
650
600
550
700
500
Refuge hut
Cheviot Burn
450
400
5. Long, tough descent
4. Left for The Schil, right for The Cheviot
Auchope Rigg
Score Head
3. Long, tough climb
350
King's Seat
531
2. Stick to fence. No problem navigating
fort
250
300
Clennel Street
Kelsocleuch
Kelsocleuch Burn
Path down to Cocklawfoot
1. Continue east and recross border fence onto slabbed path
Windy Gyle
Russell's Cairn
619
Windy Rigg
Mossy Law
BORDER
Path for Coquet Valley to Trows & Barrowburn

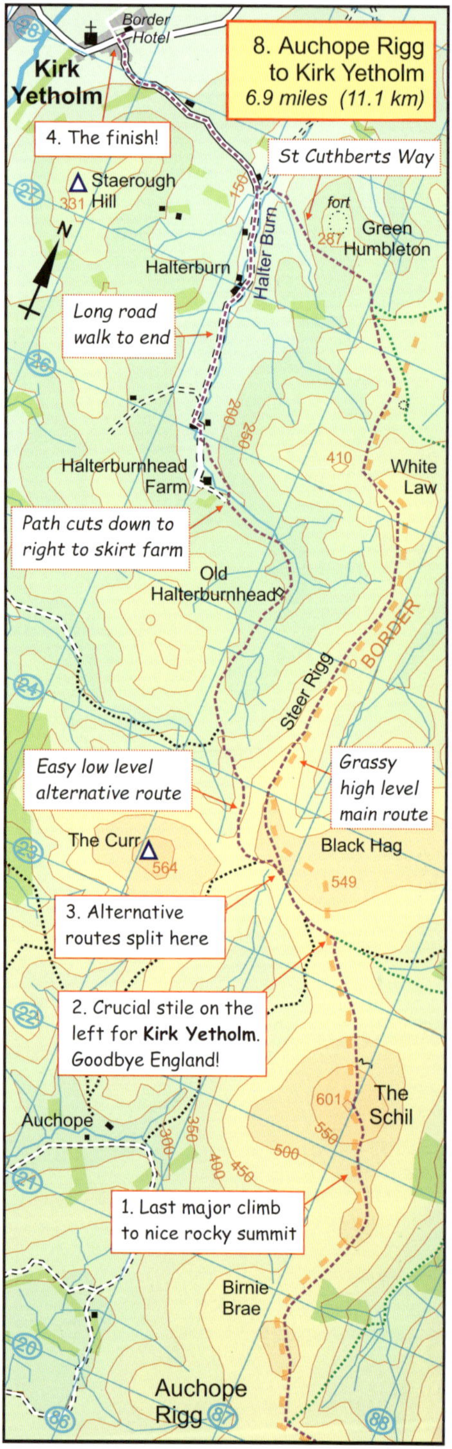
8. Auchope Rigg to Kirk Yetholm
6.9 miles (11.1 km)
Border Hotel
Kirk Yetholm
4. The finish!
St Cuthberts Way
Staerough Hill
331
fort
287
Green Humbleton
N
Halterburn
Halter Burn
Long road walk to end
200
250
410
Halterburnhead Farm
White Law
Path cuts down to right to skirt farm
Old Halterburnhead
BORDER
Steer Rigg
Easy low level alternative route
Grassy high level main route
The Curr
564
Black Hag
549
3. Alternative routes split here
2. Crucial stile on the left for Kirk Yetholm. Goodbye England!
601
The Schil
550
500
Auchope
300
350
400
450
1. Last major climb to nice rocky summit
Birnie Brae
Auchope Rigg